Stolen Moment

Part Two

Dear Derrick

Second Chance Publishing

Contents

Author Q & A

Where did you get the stories to write this book?

About 15 years ago I came up with the idea to make this a movie. I started a blog asking anyone that was sexually abused to share their story for book and or movie purposes. I received an overwhelming response in such a short period of time. I chose only five stories, to share but I have so many more. That's why I think this should be a series so we can share everyone's story.

How does PTSD affect your life?

PTSD affects me while I'm asleep, I violently fight in my sleep.

Why do you think that is?

Oh, I know why, but that's a topic for a different day.

Did you make this book in audiobook?

Yes, it comes in audible as well. I think the audiobook is absolutely incredible. The narrator did a fantastic job.

What are the projects are you working on?

Well, I have a 3 more books in the works , Stole Moment part two , Dear Derrick and the third is a relationship book. I haven't decided on a title yet.

Do you have a mentor in the film industry and or in the book industry?

It's funny you ask that, I never thought I would be a journalist or an author. No one ever taught me how to write a book. I just figured it out on my own and here we are …

So, you did not hire ghost writer to write this book for you?

No, I wrote every single word myself!!! As far as the movie industry goes, I used to be an independent Director with a film company – New Era pictures. My mentor is a guy I'm still in close communication with. He's like a brother to me, his name is GuGu E, Michaels.

What did you learn writing this book?

I learned that most people that are sexually assaulted has never reported it, because of the humiliation and shame. I want to be the voice for all those people that do not have the courage to ask for help, I will stand with you, together we can make a difference!

What is the meaning of the title stolen moment?

A stolen moment is one someone takes from you - that is irreplaceable, and that moment changed your life forever ... it's never too late to make the right decision and it's never too late to hold my hand. Let me fight for you. Let me be your voice of awareness into God's grace - together we can heal your heart.

Chapter One

New assignment

ANGER, AS DEFINED BY the Oxford dictionary: is a strong feeling of extreme displeasure. Kathryn Thacker knew it was much more than that. She knew it was the trigger for violence and abuse, and often was the result of abuse or trauma. It was the root of hatred and the cause of much of the bigotry and social unrest experienced in the world today. Kathryn also knew anger was a developed trait - not inherent or hereditary. She knew there were numerous social occurrences that could bring the anger to a violent rage in an uncontrolled second. Kathryn, herself, had been a recipient of anger. As a child her father, an alcoholic, often beat her mother. Witnessing the violent temper and uncontrolled rage led Kathryn on a quest to both learn about this horrific characteristic, as well as do something initiative-taking to heal it.

Studying psychology in college, earning advanced degrees in human behavior and social counseling meant Kathryn was highly qualified to tackle the growing angst that families and society were encountering. She had one significant problem, however. Anger frightened her. Her husband was not abusive, and her children were docile and well behaved, but just the memories of the violence she had grown up with were enough to keep her always cautious for another eruption by someone. As much as she tried to be calm, as hard as she worked to understand the nuances of angry eruptions, as practiced as she was in the linguistic art that had proven effective in controlling anger and treating those possessed of it - Kathryn Thacker couldn't control the accelerated heart rate, the sweaty palms, and the panicky feelings she experienced whenever she had to confront anger.

The images of her father's unbridled rage rose swiftly to the surface in the presence of someone in the throes of a fit of anger. For that reason, Kathryn had been reluctant to accept any assignment that put her in direct contact with angry individuals. Though her family could use the extra money she would earn by mentoring anger management classes, her husband had voiced his concern and strongly requested that she not get involved in that aspect of her studies. "This is something you need to do," Dr. Stephenson, the court appointed director for mandated anger management classes told her. "It's the next progression in your career. You have been doing research long enough." "I'm just not sure," Kathryn mumbled. "I know the money would be nice ... but my husband ... you know how he feels about me teaching a class like this." She could already feel the anxiety level spike as she thought about being in front of so many with such deep anger issues.

"Listen," Dr. Stephenson said, moving around the desk and sitting on the corner, directly in front of her. "These are all men and women who have been arrested for something they did that was precipitated by their anger. They either go to this class and pass it - or they go to jail. No middle ground here. We're not talking about people who are enrolled because their spouse is fed up with them. These are desperate folks - desperate to stay on this side of the prison bars. They will do whatever they must, and that means displaying their best behavior - or off to jail they go. You couldn't have a better group to facilitate ... to cut your teeth on - so to speak." Kathryn's eyes darted from Dr. Stephenson's lap a half a dozen times while she wrung her hands together. Her soft brown hair bobbed against her cheek. This was something she wanted to do, but she did not want to go against her husband's wishes, and the very thought of it frightened her immensely.

"You really think I can do it?" she asked, fidgeting nervously. "I know you can," Dr. Stephenson answered. "You have been studying all these years just for this moment." "But ... but what if," Kathryn stammered "what if they see that I'm frightened?" "Don't show them you're frightened," Dr. Stephenson said, as if his answer was completely logical. "Hah!" Kathryn forced a laugh "that's easy for you to say. You've been doing this for years and besides, you're a man." "What does gender have to do with it?" Dr. Stephenson chuckled, shaking his head. "You women blame everything on gender. Why is that?" Kathryn glared at him. "Because men are the aggressors. Always have been. I have read and studied this stuff for years and I know ... " Dr. Stephenson cut her off. "And that is exactly why you are perfect!" for this class, Kathryn.

"The wise counselor had no desire to engage his attractive protege in a gender war. His job was to execute the mandates of the court - to conduct the judge's orders - and to develop Kathryn Thacker into a qualified therapist. "You need this class as much as the students do," he said. "You're perfect and you're prepared mentally better than anyone I've ever known. But eventually the warrior must go into the trenches. It's time, Kathryn." Her demeanor softened. "I want to ... but." "No buts," Dr. Stephenson covered her small trembling hand with one of his. "Judge O'Brien hand selected these participants. He is giving them a second chance, and you're their vehicle to freedom. Teach them what you know. They'll love you for it."

After a short pause and a lengthy sigh, she finally said, "OK, I'll ... I'll do it." "That a girl," Dr. Stephenson beamed. "Now," the doctor snatched a thick folder from the desktop behind him and flipped it open, pulling out the first packet - a profile of one of the prospective class members, "Let me tell you about your students."

Chapter Two

Stolen moment

"GOOD MORNING, WAYNE," THE elderly priest greeted the 12-year-old boy as he checked in to the Boy's Camp. "I'm Father Peterson. I am so glad to see you. I have been waiting for your arrival." Wayne Wade was blonde haired, small built and slender, with eyes so blue they appeared nearly transparent and, he was handsome. He had been told that since he was a child. "Such a striking boy," ladies would tell his mother. And men would comment how "ruggedly good looking the lad is." His first-grade teacher called him "the cutest, best-behaved boy in the class." Since his father's sudden death, 3 years ago, Wayne had been more trouble than anything else. Having the police show up at their front door with Wayne in tow was becoming a regular occurrence for Lisa Wade, Wayne's mother.

As a 31-year-old single mom, Lisa struggled in every area of her life, and having a delinquent son drove her close to tears every night. "He was throwing rocks at the neighbor's windows," the officer told her the first time he was escorted home. That was a minor infraction compared to the events that followed. Angry at the world for taking his father from him, Wayne attracted fights as fast as he attracted love-sick girls, which was constantly. Fighting, vandalism, shoplifting - Wayne was a menace and a nuisance, and he was never repentant.

"I've scheduled you to go to a camp," Lisa told her son as they left Juvenile Court ... again. Wayne had been seated in the hallway for 30 minutes while his mother worked out a compromise with the Courts. "The Judge says I won't have to pay for all the damage you caused if you just go to this camp. I cannot afford to keep paying for your actions," Lisa wasn't irate, she was trying to be calm and loving. But Wayne's behavior had stretched her like a tug-o-war rope. Her love for her only child pulling tight at her heart strings while his behavior was jerking her emotions the other way.

"Fine by me." Wayne shrugged. He knew girls loved to be around him. He knew he would get out of whatever mess he was in - eventually - somehow. Hell, hadn't he already finagled a way around paying for all the damage his latest escapade caused? If it meant going to some stupid camp for the summer, he would do it. Sure, he'd miss his mom, but she seemed relieved to be getting rid of him for a while. And he'd surely find some new ways to have fun once he got to the camp. Lisa drove him, the ride a solemn, silent trek up into the foothills of North Texas. "Wayne, honey," she finally spoke as the station wagon eased into the parking lot, "please don't be upset at me. I love you, sweetheart."

"I'm not upset," Wayne sounded irritated at the statement. "If this is what you want me to do, I'll do it." His sullenness was not lost on his mother. She felt he was resigning himself to his fate rather than looking at this as a second chance. "It's not what I want," Lisa stopped the car and looked directly at her son. "It's what the Court wants - it's what we have to do." Wayne shrugged his shoulders. "Then I will do it, no big deal."

"You're nearly a man now, honey," Lisa was clutching his hands, desperate to find a way to bring back the cheerful boy who changed so dramatically when his father died ... or was it when they moved repeatedly ... ever since she had become a widow ... or was it the lack of money. Lisa worked as much as she could but being a teacher was long hours for little pay. Whatever the reason, she was praying that this time at the camp would be different, that it would bring him back from his anger and alienation. "I know the speech, Mom," Wayne snapped. "I will be a good boy." "Oh, Wayne," Lisa sighed heavily, "I love you." She leaned across the seat and kissed his forehead. "I really do." "And I love you, too, Mom,"

Wayne yanked open the door, lifted his box of clothing from the back seat, and walked away. Wayne didn't turn around, but he heard the station wagon back up and rattle away. He glanced up at the foreboding door of the administration building, took a deep breath, then entered. Camp wasn't what Wayne had expected. Just the word 'camp' sounded so primitive. This camp, however, was modern with indoor plumbing and hot showers. And instead of skills he anticipated learning - how to pitch a tent or cook over an open fire - the curriculum here was centered around the Bible. The spacious chapel was the most prominent building on the campus. It was there that Wayne Wade met Father Murphy.

"How are you liking the camp, son?" the younger priest asked him as he sat on a pew reading from the bible. Wayne had been at the camp for more than a week. He enjoyed the soccer games and the evening discussions, but the serenity of the chapel was his favorite place to be. "I'm doing fine sir," Wayne responded. "I like the camp a lot, more than I thought I would." "My name is Father Murphy," the priest smiled. Father Murphy was 41 years old and on the fast track to becoming a bishop or even a cardinal. Many in the upper echelons of the church's hierarchy had noticed his valiant services.

"I knew your father," the genteel clergyman told the young boy. "My Dad? Really?" Wayne sat up, closed the Bible, and turned his full attention to Father Murphy. "Oh, yes," the Priest nodded. "We both came here as boys. We were best friends." "Can you tell me about him ... about my dad?" Wayne's entire countenance lit up. The priest smiled warmly. "Of course, my son. We'll have plenty of time for that." He patted Wayne softly on the knee. "I think you and I will become very good friends, too."

At the soccer field several days later, Wayne slid to make a kick and felt a sharp pain in the back of his leg. "I think it could be your hamstring," Father Peterson said after a cursory examination on the sidelines. "Why don't you go see Father Murphy," the older priest pointed to the building. "He's in the locker room. He can help you." When Wayne hobbled into the locker room, Father Murphy immediately sat him down on the massage table. Hoping to discuss some more about his father, Wayne first showed the priest where his leg hurt. He responded with a sharp wince when Father Murphy touched the tender part of his thigh. "Relax," the priest told him. "Let me check it out for you." "I hope it's not serious," Wayne said as Father Murphy ran his hand gently up Wayne's leg, massaging and feeling. "How does that feel?" he asked, massaging deeper. "Better," Wayne admitted.

When Father Murphy ran his hand up under Wayne's shorts, the boy jerked. "Easy," Father Murphy grinned. "I'm just checking out your hamstring. You want to feel better, don't you?" "Uh huh," the startled boy answered. "Then relax. I know what God wants and how He will make you feel better. Just lay down on your back. I'll do the rest." Haltingly, Wayne laid back, resting his head on the small pillow, while the priest stroked him. Occasionally Wayne would gasp, but his anxiety kept him from saying anything or stopping the Priest's actions "Your father and I used to help each other this way, when we were boys," Father Murphy said, still rubbing him. The mention of his father calmed Wayne down some and he lay still. "Does that feel good?" Father Murphy asked. "Uh huh," Wayne admitted, stammering out the words. "Good," the priest sounded so soft, kind, comforting. "I know what I'm doing son. You will see."

When they left the locker room, moments later, the spasm in Wayne's leg was relieved. His leg felt better, but his confusion was extreme. He had never felt such a sensation before. "Father Murphy," the timid young lad looked up at the tall man. "What was that white stuff" "That was the pain leaving your body, son. Did it make you feel better?" Wayne thought a minute, remembering. "Yeah, I guess so." "That's just the beginning my boy. I'll teach you how to really be a man - how to make everything feel better - how you can help me feel better - how to please God." The Father looped his arm around Wayne as they walked. "You think you're ready for that?" Wayne didn't answer. He just kept walking and Father Murphy kept embracing him and the other boys kept staring at him.

Chapter Three

Silent voice that cried for help

"OH, STOP!" KATHRYN ALMOST wept. "How could anyone do that to a boy?" "He had gone to the camp - to the care of men who took advantage of him." The doctor spoke slowly, trying to give Kathryn a sense of the devastation that had wrecked Wayne's life. "Instead of curing the anger he had within him, from his father's death ... he cultivated a deeper anger ... an anger that molded him into the person you'll have in your class." "I ... I'm almost afraid to ask," Kathryn said. "What did he do to get in trouble with the court?" Dr. Stephenson closed the file on his lap and looked at his young counselor. "Kathryn," he asked, "do you have any concept ... any idea what something like this would do to a kid?!" Kathryn shook her head. "Only what I've read about in test books," she said.

"Father Murphy told him - repeatedly - that he would be punished severely if he ever told anyone. That God would punish him and his mother - that no one would believe him because Father Murphy was a priest and, maybe worst of all, that his mother and everyone around him would hate him and ridicule him and, in the end, call him a liar." Kathryn moaned. "He turned to crime, didn't he?" "He's in the class, Kathryn," the doctor reminded her, "because he has a problem with his anger, not his criminal behavior. Any overt act he committed was a direct result of the anger he felt - anger at Father Murphy for what he made him do ... anger at himself for allowing it ... and anger at God for taking his father and for leaving him so vulnerable and unprotected.

As much as he tried to keep it a secret, a dirty, dark secret - because Father Murphy was molesting many other boys, the word got out and Wayne was mocked and called some horrific names. He tried to retaliate - to defend himself when he was taunted - he was finally expelled from the school for fighting and poor performance - but not before Father Murphy issued him one final warning - one that left him shaken and hurt and feeling cheap. He had been abused in the most destructive manner and all that weighed down on him as he made the move to a new school ... again." "So," Kathryn's soft eyes were pleading for the boy she had never met. "What happened ... what did he do?"

Chapter Four

In shock

KATHRYN LOOKED AT DR. Stephenson, who looked up from the file. "Did ... did this you know ... continue?" The doctor pressed his jaw tightly together and nodded. "Not only did it continue, but it accelerated." "Accelerated?" Kathyrn scrunched up her face. "How long was he at the camp?" "That's just it," Dr. Stephenson tapped the file with his index finger. "Father Murphy convinced the court and the church that Wayne had done so well at the camp but that all the progress could unravel quickly if he were allowed to go back to public school." Kathyrn's eyes widened, and her mouth dropped open. "He ... the priest ...this Father Murphy he ..." The therapist nodded. "He convinced them Wayne needed to be in Catholic school - the Catholic school where he was an administrator where he had close contact with the students, including Wayne, every day." Kathryn clutched her arms around herself and shuddered, as if she were cold. The doctor paused a moment then looked back down at the file and continued to read.

Chapter Five

Behind closed doors

"**Y**OU'RE NEW HERE, AREN'T you?" one of the girls, a classmate, had spent a week getting up the courage to talk to Wayne Wade. "Yeah," Wayne said, impressed that one of the most attractive girls in school had approached him. Before the conversation even started it was interrupted. "Father Murphy would like to see you in his office, Mr. Wade," the matronly nun announced loudly. When Wayne hesitated, she barked, "He means immediately, young man!" Wayne gave a quick smile and a nod to the girl, then hustled out the door and down the hall. "Come in," the priest called when Wayne tapped on his office door. "You wanted to see me, Father?" "Yes, I did," Father Murphy was sitting behind a large desk, his hands interlocked as they rested on the desktop. He slowly rose from his chair, casually walked across the room to lock the door.

When he finally reseated himself with such nonchalance it seemed to Wayne that this is normal. The priest asked, "How do you like your new start ... your new school?" Wayne was still processing what he had seen. "Uh ... good, I guess," he managed to say. Father Murphy grinned. "That's wonderful. I know your mother was incredibly pleased and excited for this new beginning and the tuition which I arranged to be paid. You were pleased, too, weren't you?" "Uh, yes sir," he mumbled. "Thank you, sir." "I knew you needed to be here," the priest said, so calmly and casually. "We will become good friends, just as your father and I did when he was here. Wayne nodded, his mind cluttered, his palms sticky.

"Why don't you come around here, Wayne," the priest motioned rolling his chair away from the desk "we can talk better if you're closer. I have some things I want to show you ... and teach you." As if on autopilot, Wayne robotically stood and did as he was instructed. Father Murphy wiggled in his chair, and when Wayne went around the desk, he saw Father Murphy's pants unzipped and he was fondling himself. He was sitting at the desk, his legs apart, his nakedness apparent, Wayne sucked in a jerky breath and his body went rigid. Afraid and nervous, he had never before seen a grown man naked.

"It's OK," Father Murphy said in a tender, kind voice. "This is what I wanted to show you ... what I want to teach you, the way to please God ... to make Him proud of you and want to bless you and your mother. You do want God to bless you, don't you, Wayne?" Wayne nodded. His head moving slowly up and down, his eyes fixed on the floor. "Come over here," Father Murphy took his hand, tugging him forward, placing him between his legs. "I'll teach you how to please God through me - then I'll please God through you."

Father Murphy placed a hand on Wayne's shoulder and pushed him to kneel. When Wayne was crouched in front of the priest, kneeling under the large desk, the clergyman pressed his erection into Wayne's face. "Kiss it," he almost whispered. "God wants you to kiss it." Wayne tentatively did as he was told - lightly touching his lips to the man's penis. "Oh, no," the man was sterner. "You are mocking God now. Take it - in – kiss it hard - with your mouth open - let it go inside. That's what pleases God the most." As he watched, a frightened Wayne tried to obey the man he trusted... the man who had been his father's best friend for many years he claimed to be God's servant. The priest pushed on the back of Wayne's head, forcing it down onto his erection. Wayne gagged. "Yes," Father Murphy moaned. "Like that ... deep and hard."

Chapter Six

Abuse to violence

"MY NAME IS ALYSSA," the perky brunette in a cheerleader outfit, wearing an ear-to-ear grin, said jamming a hand towards Wayne. "I know you're new to our school. Hope you like it." "Are you the official welcoming committee?" Wayne asked, shaking her hand. "You only find out that answer if you meet me after school," Alyssa winked. "'Cuz I got to get to class now ... and so do you. Meet me at my locker at 3:00." She pulled the pen from Wayne's pocket and wrote on his hand '1327' "That's my locker number. First floor, you will find it." Then she bounced away. Wayne did not take his eyes off her until she rounded the corner at the end of the hallway. "What just happened?" he mumbled to himself, grinning, looking at the ink marks on his hand. '1327' and a little heart. "I think I'm gonna like it here." The anger that had coiled inside him like a lurking serpent subsided.

His step had an extra bounce in it as he bounded off for his next class. Alyssa was waiting at her locker - just as she said she would be - at 3:00. "So, Mr. New Kid, uh, Wayne Wade ... I asked around and found out your name ... what school did you come from?" Alyssa wasn't a cheerleader because of her athletic abilities - she was a cheerleader because she was a looker- stunning, very mature physically, and gregarious. She could easily have passed for a college student or even a magazine model. "I went to a catholic school," Wayne confessed. "Other side of town." "But it's the middle of the year," Alyssa was walking close enough to him that their bodies brushed up against each other as they took each step.

"Did your family move?" "It's just me and my mom," Wayne told her. "And we didn't move – I got kicked out." "Kicked out!" Alyssa snapped her head back to look at him. "What for? I thought the bad boys were sent to catholic school." "Fighting," Wayne said, quickly remembering the reasons for the fights, his stomach nearly wrenching when his mind saw Father Murphy. "Oh," Alyssa smiled and nudged closer. "A real bad boy. I think I like that." Wayne raised an eyebrow. "You like bad boys?" The cute girl looked out of the tops of her eyes. "Only if he can get really bad - if you know what I mean."

Alyssa slipped her arm through his and snuggled closer. When word got around that Wayne, the new kid, was dating Alyssa Jacobs - the hottest girl in the school - every girl fell in love with him ... every boy was jealous of him ... and every person wanted to know more about this new kid that was taking over the school. Somehow, someone contacted a student from the Catholic school and rumors began to circulate faster than a gulf coast hurricane. In the locker room during gym class, Wayne noticed a group of boys huddled up, pointing at him, and laughing as he changed his clothing. The calmness he had felt for three weeks began to crumble. It had been 3 weeks of being with Alyssa every night making out, feeling sensations that ignited his passions - sensations that felt natural, fun, and delicious. Not like the demeaning, filthy things Father Murphy made him do ... the things he saw every night in his sleep.

Allysa never heard the rumors, or if she did, she was careful to never mention them to Wayne. Her main concern was keeping him away from other girls who flocked around him like gulls on a fishing boat. "Let's go to my house," the pert cheerleader said as they left school, holding hands. "Your house?" Wayne scrunched up his face. "I don't think your dad likes me ... and I know your mom doesn't." "She's not home, neither of them are." She squeezed his hand tighter. "Besides, it's not you. She thinks we 're screwing and she doesn't' want me to get pregnant." "Screwing?" Wayne sounded shocked. "Why would she think that?" "Don't know, " Alyssa shrugged. "But if she's gonna think it, why disappoint her?"

She pressed a condom into Wayne's hand. Wayne looked down at the sealed package, his eyes popping open his heart leaping in his chest. "You mean it?" he said softly. "I wanted this since I first met you," she said. "I figured you did too, but you needed a push," she gave him a loving nudge, "So whadya say, my house?" Wayne grinned. "Oh yeah ... your house it is." The act of having sex was supposed to be thrilling - to be liberating and satisfying. Wayne wanted it to be all that and more. This was his first-time having sex.

He did not ever want to see Father Murphy's face--his naked-ness-- every time he looked at Alyssa. The more he tried to lose himself in Alyssa, the more his memories tormented him. Her soft voluptuous body - the curves - the tender areas that stimulated him - were fighting with the horrid memories of what had occurred in the priest's office. When Alyssa tried to show him love in ways he desired, doing things he knew he should enjoy, he could squeeze his eyes shut as tight as a sealed jar ... but he could not shut out the haunting images. Afterwards, when he should have felt that unique euphoria,

Wayne instead grappled with a temper that seemed on the edge - ready to lash out.

More than a month after their first time sleeping together, Alyssa convinced Wayne to rent a motel room. "You're always so tense, baby," she told him. "I think you're worried about my parents coming home." Wayne could not discuss the real reason for his anxiety, he couldn't tell her about the demons that possessed him each time he got an erection - could not even talk about the taunting he received from those at school who had heard about his liaisons with the priest. "You'll relax in a motel room," Alyssa cooed in his ear, nibbling on the lobe as he drove. Wayne nodded. "Maybe you're right." "I know I am." She sounded so much more excited. She pressed his hand to her breasts. "You'll find these a lot more fun when you're relaxed."

Wayne sped up, risking a ticket to get to the motel room faster, hoping this would be the answer he was looking for. Alyssa had been correct. For some reason Wayne was having a lot more fun in the motel room -- enjoying everything they did together, until he climaxed. The sensation brought only a rush of guilt and humiliation and he sprung from the bed and rushed into the tiny bathroom. Alyssa had no such regrets. She lay, naked, on the bed, her breathing heavy and deep. The sweat on her body glistened under the motel room light. Her entire body tingled with satisfaction. Then Wayne's phone began to ring. Alyssa casually picked it up and instantly recognized the incoming number.

When Wayne finally emerged from the bathroom, Alyssa was furious. "Why the hell is Sheila Dawson calling you?" she growled. Wayne snapped. "You lookin' at my phone?" he yelled. "It rang!" She yelled back, just as loud "I was gonna bring it to you... Then I saw her number. Why is she calling you?" "Don't ever touch my phone!" Wayne grabbed it from her shoving her back onto the bed. "Don't touch me," Alyssa screamed. "You use me and then think you can dump me and go off screwin' Sheila Dawson. Is that why you are so lousy in bed with me?" All Wayne could see was Father Murphy -- threatening him -- warning him.

His anger raged. The repeated abuse, the taunting, the overwhelming guilt - all rose in one volcanic fury. "I'll do whatever I want!" he hollered back at Alyssa. "Don't ever tell me what to do!" Alyssa was kneeling on the bed as Wayne leaned into her, spit flying from his rabid mouth as he spoke. "You son of a ..." Alyssa flailed her arms, slapping at him. Her tantrum released his years of pent-up aggression and Wayne exploded. In a reflexive response, he backhanded Alyssa hard across the face, knocking her from her kneeling position - up against the headboard. Her hands flew instantly to her face, the pain ricocheting through her head - her eyeball throbbing - her vision blurry. "You hit me!" she moaned when her voice came back - tears streaming down her cheeks.

Already her eye was swelling and changing color. "Get the hell out of here!" She yelled at him between sobs. "Get out and never touch me again." Wayne obeyed. He slammed the door so hard when he left that the lamp on the little table toppled over and crashed on the floor. As much as she tried to hide it from her parents, Alyssa's Mom discovered the badly bruised cheek and eye. "My God!" she screamed when she spun her daughter around. "Who did that to you? Did that Wayne kid do this?" Alyssa's tears gushed out again as if her mom's words had broken some imaginary dam holding them back. "I'm calling the cops!" Mrs. Jacobs said. "NO, Mom, no!" Alyssa wept, grabbing for the phone. Her mother jerked it away and shook her head. "Your father is going to flip out when he sees your eye. He is going to kill that boy!" She dialed 9-1-1 and reported the crime.

Chapter Seven

Anger management

KATHRYN WAS HOLDING HER elbows in her palms, her head moving slowly back and forth. Dr. Stephenson looked up from the file. "He'll be a challenge to reach," the doctor promised ... warning her. "The boy was hurt, and no one has rescued him. His blood runs on anger right now." Kathryn was nearly speechless. "Such ..." She gathered her thoughts. "Such a tragic life." She took a deep breath, then added, "I guess every class has a hard story like that." Dr. Stephenson half chuckled, though nothing was funny, "You have ten people scheduled to attend the class, he tapped the stack of files. "I'm not sure Wayne's story is any worse than the others," Kathryn gasped. "You mean ... all of them ... have been abused like he was?"

"In some form or another, yes." the doctor nodded "That's why their anger is out of control. That is why they need what you know and the benefit of the tools you have studied and learned. This is their best chance their last chance before prison takes hold of them." "But ... sexually abused ... by a priest!" Kathryn shuddered again, her hair flipping across her ashen face. "He trusted that man ... he was a friend of his fathers. Oh my gosh!" She could not force out the words - simply clamped a hand to her mouth. When she regained her composure, she asked, "You don't think ... his father and the priest." Dr. Stephson waited a moment before answering. "We know Wayne's Dad was friends with Father Murphy - childhood friends. More than that is only speculation. But what we know for certainty is that Wayne needs our help - needs your help. As do all the others in the class."

Dr Stephenson reaches for his next file and begins talking about Sam. A 55-year-old man who started drinking after he lost his wife. He was struggling to cope with the lot that life had given him, and in his mind, the bottle was the only option. One drunken night he went to the liquor store look-ing for his favorite flavor to escape. When he was told they were out, that was the match igniting the ticking timebomb that Sam had become. Sam started screaming uncontrollably "YOU STUPID MOTHERFUCKERS! HOW CAN YOU RUN OUT OF MAD DOG 20/20!!" Sam grabbed a liter of vodka and threw it at the clerk, barely missing his head. "DUMBASS!" The clerk ducked for cover. Sam then started throwing bottle after bottle of other liquors smashing them on the floor. The fear of his reality had become too much, and he exploded. He needed to feel the smooth silk feeling that consumed his throat when he drank his favorite liquor. He knew just how much it would take to elude his reality. Sam managed to destroy over $4000 of alcohol before the police were able to subdue him.

"There are some who have been struggling with this issue most of their lives. You have broken spouses, ex-prisoners and angry fathers, wives of cheating husbands and victims of gang rapes. Their stories are tragic - each and every one of them – but" Dr. Stephenson pinched Kathryn's chin with his thumb and index finger, forcing her to look at him, "Each one of them is curable! Judge O'Brien would not have put them in the class, keeping them out of jail, unless he felt they could be cured." Kathryn's eyes shone fear, but she motioned her head up and down in a show of confidence. "You need to do this, Kathryn," he said, still holding her chin. "For each person in this class - and that means you, too." "I will try," she murmured. "And I'll be here to support you. Now, ready to hear about the rest of your students?" Kathryn raised her upper lip. "I guess so," she whined.

Chapter Eight

Determined

I T TOOK DR. STEPHENSON a little more. than 2 hours to discuss the data in his folder with Kathryn. Armed with her abundance of classroom training and a cursory sketch of each of the students - based on the information in their files - Kathryn Thacker spent her final night before tackling the anger management class attempting to diffuse the simmering irritation her husband was experiencing. Despite his objections and stern disapproval, Kathryn had accepted the job, which would take her out of the home four nights per week for 12 weeks. "We need the money," Kathryn tried to justify her decision.

"No!" Herb Thacker shook his head. "Extra money would be nice, but we don't NEED it. It's not mandatory." "Christmas." Kathryn floundered, "I'm doing this for ... us ... and them." Her emotions seemed tied up in knots inside her. "You're certainly not doing this for US!" Herb's voice was elevated. "To leave me and our daughter - every night - don't try to say this is for us!" Kathryn was near tears, but she kept her composure, wondering what kind of a teacher she would be if she fell apart in front of her husband - before she even taught one class. "If I do this class," she haltingly said, "my reputation will grow and then I can lead day classes and be home at night and make more money."

Herb turned away. Looking out the big window in their front room. "I still don't like it. You know nothing about these people or ... " "Oh but," she interrupted. "They have anger issues, but I would too if my life had been like theirs." Herb could feel the compassion in her voice, it was one of the reasons he had fallen in love with her. Reluctantly, he faced her again ... and listened. "Jennifer, a 19-year-old girl," Kathryn began, leaning forward with her eyes pleading for his understanding. "She was drugged and gang raped by a group of university frat boys who recorded it and distributed the video around campus. And Herb ... it was Jennifer, the victim, who was kicked out of school!"

Kathryn continued, "Can you believe that? Who wouldn't develop an anger issue after being treated like that ... the reason she was assigned to this class to begin with - is because when she attempted to leave campus after being humiliated by the video of her abuse, Kyle and Little Buddy started antagonizing her ... to the point of following her down the interstate in their jeep, hanging out the window making sexual jesters and laughing at her. The more she tried to avoid them the harder they worked to ruin her life ... after several desperate attempts to get away from them and could not, she exploded! It just so happened that it took place in front of a highway police officer who was monitoring the streets! She was outraged, and took matters into her own hands by using her car as a weapon, running Kyle off the road causing him to lose control of his jeep and crashing ... because of those boys, her life has spiraled out of control. She needs someone to offer a hand of help. Someone to be on her side Herb! We can help her! I can help her get her life back!"

Herb was working his jaw muscles tenaciously. "That's just one girl." he muttered, sucking his teeth, and grinding them. "What about the others? How many are dangerous?" Kathryn was now growing stronger by Herb's questions and his concern. She felt she had ammunition to convince him this was not only a good decision, but a decision she had to make because of her training. "You mean like Maybeth Simmons?" Kathryn asked, letting the name linger in the air a moment. "You might recognize the name," she suggested as Herb's eyebrows furrowed. "She is the wife of the city councilman who was arrested for molesting their daughter...

the same daughter who committed suicide because she felt so helpless and could not stop her own father from abusing her."

Kathryn paused to let the thought grow. "Are you able to think of anything more repulsive ... or feel anything but anger for the man just from hearing the story? Imagine how that poor girl and how her mother must have felt to live through it." Herb blinked, the tragedy of the situations sinking deep in him. But he was speaking in a near whisper, "Couldn't any of them ... maybe not the ones ... the abused ones ... but any of the others ... couldn't they become violent? After all, anger is the root of violence, is it not?" He half smiled as he quoted one of his wife's often repeated mantras. "Yes," Kathryn replied. "It is. And I suppose Brian is the most likely to act out his anger. But I doubt he will. He will learn from this too..." "What did this Brian do?" Herb stopped her, his eyes widening as his wife admitted there was a chance violence could break out in the class.

"Brian has several incidents of attacking people," Kathryn calmly repeated Dr. Stephenson's analysis. "For a variety of reasons. But I wouldn't call him dangerous." "He attacked people!" Herb nearly shouted. "How could that NOT be dangerous?" "Well," Kathryn held her ground, recalling her similar reaction when Dr. Stephenson told her about Brian, she kept her head high and her eyes fixed on her husband - a posture Herb had never seen his wife take. "Brian was provoked. For example, one time he was defending a girl. Actually it was Jennifer. He was there when she was attacked. He knew them and tried to stop it. But he feared that his football scholarship would be revoked if he was involved so he left. He was trying to keep those men from harassing her. When the men continued, Brian took after them to protect the girl. In his eyes he was doing the right thing. And there were other times - other provocations. I am not saying violence is justified ... it never is," she quickly said. "But when you grow up around it, sometimes you feel that violence is the only way to get your point across or getting what you need."

Kathryn paused, then said, "It's my job to show him there is a better way." Herb's shoulders slumped slightly. He could see the strong determination Kathryn had. For years he had witnessed his highly educated wife flounder in a mediocre position that did not utilize her knowledge and her training. He wanted her to succeed - but he also knew the fragility her past had created, and he wanted, more than anything else, to protect her. More than his desire to have her home each night, Herb feared for his wife. If something happened where Kathryn was the victim of violence - again - he was afraid she would break ... or shatter. And shattered objects are nearly impossible to put back together.

Herb knew his wife was determined. "OK," Herb covered her small hands with one of his large palms. "But I want you to give me a complete report every night of everything that happens in your class, because some of these folks still sound dangerous - and you have not even told me about all of them yet." "Oh, I will, dear," Kathryn gushed. "I promise! She squeezed his hand tightly, her face breaking into a wide smile." "I'm still going to worry about you." Herb maintained his stoic countenance. "Every moment you're gone I will be worried and anxious until you get home." "And I love you for that." Kathryn told him. "But I'll be fine. You'll see." She smiled wider, then jumped to her feet and clutched him around the waist, hugging him close. "This will be our very best Christmas ever!" she promised, alluding to the extra money she would earn. "Like the song says," He whispered into her ear. "All I want for Christmas is you!"

Chapter Nine

A good friend

D R. STEPHENSON SAT FOR a long time staring out the window of his office. At night he could see the skyline lights of Dallas twinkling in the distance, while below him, in the darkened streets, he knew the seedy side of humanity was acting itself out in a variety of nefarious ways. On any other night, he would often sit at the window, his fingers surrounding the bowl of his pipe, lamenting that he couldn't march down among the gangs, the drug dealers, the pimps and burglars and loop his arm around and them tell them he loved them - pull them off the highway that was rapidly taking them to a life of misery or worse a very shortened life.

Tonight, was different - yes. The doctor's heart ached for the wasted lives and the lost potential he knew was out there. But tonight, his thoughts were on one person Kathryn Thacker. Had he the thrown her into the deep end of the pool before she could swim? Was she strong enough to handle the tragic stories she would surely hear? She nearly broke down just listening to the details in the files. What if someone acted up? What would Kathryn do if one of her students challenged her techniques? How would she handle a failure? Someone who refused to change and ended up in prison? Would she blame herself? With a jerk, Dr. Stephenson swiveled in his chair, grabbed his rolodex, and found the name that had just popped into his head.

The man answered on the third ring. "Dr. Fuquan." the deep, masculine voice said, a sense of weariness in his tone. "James, this is Clay Stephenson," the doctor lit up when he heard his old friend's voice. "Clay!" Dr. Fuquan greeted him. "So good to hear from you, my friend. To what do I owe this privilege?" "Just a friendly call," Dr. Stephenson tried to cover his real intent. "Just wondering how you are, how busy you are." "Uh-huh," Dr. Fuquan gave him his suspicious voice. "Like the last time - every time you call me. What's it going to cost me?" "Why James?" Doctor Stephenson feigned an insulted air, "When have I ever?" "When haven't you," Fuquan chuck-led. "It's either a fundraiser or a charity golf tournament or you need a last-minute guest speaker at some function. It has been what ... 6 months since we spoke. I figure you've run out of friends and I'm your last resort."

Both men laughed, but Dr. Stephenson quickly turned serious. "Actually, James, you were my first choice. I'm troubled by something, and I need your wise counsel." James Fuquan hesitated briefly, his lips smacking together. His schedule was already far overbooked, but Clay Stephenson was one of the few people he called a close friend possibly his closest. "Clay," he answered equally as serious, "you know I'll help you with anything. You are the best man I've met since I have been here. Anything you need ... any time." "Thank you, James," the mutual respect was evident in his answer. "That means a lot to me. And I wouldn't impose unless I was really concerned."

"Do you want to meet somewhere?" Fuquan offered. "I'm about to close up for the night. I can swing over to your side of town." "I'm still at the office," Stephenson informed him. "I'll be waiting for you. Doors open. Come on up." "Give me 20 minutes," Fuquan said, and hung up without another word. He arrived in fifteen, parked out front and strode quickly into the building. In the years he had known Clay Stephenson - the only man he had ever confided in - the only man who knew even the deepest, darkest secrets of James Fuquan's life - he had never heard him sound so urgent ... never heard him request they meet immediately in the middle of the night.

He would have gone anywhere for this man. The drive across town was nothing. "Come in James, Doctor Stephenson said before his colleague could knock. The door to his office was open and Dr. Stephenson was still squeezing his pipe, gazing, but not seeing, out the window. "Is everything OK, Clay?" Fuquan asked, stepping into the office and walking to the desk. "I hope so," the concerned counselor replied, swiveling his chair again to face his friend. "But I need your advice, your help." James Fuquan just nodded as he sat in front of the desk. Quickly Dr. Stephenson told his friend about the anger management class - about Judge O'Brien's offer to the ten individuals - and about Kathryn Thacker, his hand-picked classroom mentor.

Noticing the desperation and concern in his tone and facial expressions, Dr. Fuquan tapped his fingers on each hand together. "You're concerned about the girl this Kathryn ... the teacher." Stephenson nodded. "Can she handle it?" he asked, not expecting an answer. "My fear is something will happen that destroys her - and then we lose the students, too. Not sure I could live with that." Dr. Fuquan eyed his good friend, then chose his words carefully. "Clay, we can never be sure about anything or anybody. You know that as well as I do. But we can keep our fingers on the pulse of what is going on, try to monitor things in an effort to catch anything before it happens."

"That's just it," Stephenson interrupted him. "My schedule is so full. I'm doing a class at SMU the same nights Kathryn will be handling her class. Not that I would go sit in. I think that would be disastrous. She'd be nervous- She'd think I don't have faith in her – and the students would pick up on it and lose respect for her, thinking she needed a babysitter." "I understand, " Fuquan agreed. "Why don't you tell me the makeup of the class. Let's see what we have here."

Clay Stephenson grinned and sighed. "I have the files right here," he said. "I was hoping you had the time." "I'm an older, African American, single man," Dr. Fuquan returned the grin with sarcasm. "What kind of a social life do I have here in the middle of Cowboy Country?" Doctor Stephenson so appreciated his friend's self-deprecating humor. Dr. Fuquan was, he knew, a tall, strong, wealthy, and successful bachelor. He could, in reality, have any number of women. There was an endless supply of beautiful ladies who were interested. He was never short of offers.

His profession, however, was his life. Clay Stephenson knew why ... he knew James Fuquan had been hurt in the past. He understood the reasons for his solitary life, though he never gave up trying to convince him that love was the greatest delight of life. "I love my work," Dr. Fuquan would always answer. "A man can only have one true love, right?" He would joke away any further discussion about his love life.

"Besides," he would explain, "I want to keep others out of the gutters that derailed me for a while." Doctor Stephenson respected and admired the dignified psychologist too much to force the issue. After all, he wasn't sure he would be any different than his friend if he had been dealt the hand James Fuquan had lived with and overcame. "I appreciate your help, James," Dr. Stephenson said with a sincerity both men knew was real.

A little before 4:00 a.m., after hearing the cases and discussing each one, James Fuquan rose. "I'm buying breakfast," he yawned. "Then we both need a few hours of sleep. It looks like we will both be busy. You have classes to teach, I have a practice to run, and we'll both be closely following what's going on with Mrs. Kathryn." "I sure appreciate this, James," Dr. Stephenson said, the circles under his eyes feeling like they had been replaced with soothing patches. "I was just so worried." "You were right to be concerned," Fuquan. nodded. "you've got more than one powder keg in that class. The tiniest spark could ignite an explosion ... a deadly explosion."

Chapter Ten

Last chance

THE THICK, MUGGY TEXAS humidity hung on the bright, blue sky like moss on a river rock. It couldn't be classified as a heat wave - Dallas was always hot in July - but with the humidity hovering above 60% it was the kind of heat only an ice-cold water could temper. The well maintained, small church with its freshly painted white siding had been built before the country saw 1900. While the church was meticulously cared for as if it were the home of God himself, the neighborhood surrounding the little chapel had deteriorated into one of the more dangerous and seedy areas of the city. Gangs owned the streets. Most of the reputable businesses had long ago relocated, leaving the ghetto to liquor stores, pawn shops, and XXX rated peep shows.

Samuel Thomas blinked back at the effulgent sky and slipped on a pair of sunglasses, stepping out of the church and onto the sidewalk. Samuel was barely 55 years old, but he looked much older. A life of alcoholism had aged him far beyond his years. The 40-year-old man who exited with him was even worse ... his large body a result of extreme neglect, overeating, and a drunken stupor each night. "Kinda ironic, isn't it, Sam?" the younger man said, poking his chin at the flashing neon sign across the street that announced, 'LARRY'S LIQUORS.' Sam glanced at the man without speaking. Growing up as an African American in the racially charged neighborhoods of Birmingham, Alabama, Sam never accepted the notion that whites, and blacks could intermingle. He did not trust them. He'd seen too much, heard too many stories, tried too hard to drown his pains in the bottom of a bottle.

"You know," the man persisted. "Coming out of an AA meeting and the first thing we see is a liquor store. You know it kind of tests a fella's will power. Know what I mean?" Sam gave the man a cursory nod, pulled his cap down tight on his head, and walked away. "Hey," the younger man said, trying to keep pace with Sam's long strides, "Where ya headin' buddy?" The man had one eye on Sam, the other on the liquor store and his tongue was doing laps around his mouth. Sam didn't slow down. "To another meeting." he said without looking at him. "Another meeting," the man echoed. "Another AA meeting?" "Somethin' like that," Sam grumbled. "WOW, " his fellow alcoholic panted, already tired from the heat and Sam's rapid pace. "You're really tryin' to kick this thing, ain't ya? I mean, two meetings in one day. That's dedication." Sam didn't' respond. He turned left at the corner, his fellow AA member lagging behind.

Sam didn't look over his shoulder. He knew the man was no longer following him. He knew that younger man was already crossing the street. If he listened close, he was sure he'd soon hear the jingle of the bells over the door of LARRY'S LIQUORS. Sam would have done the same if it was not for old Judge O'Brien. He walked a little faster, keeping an eye on his watch. The old school was about 3 miles from the little church where he needed to be. Sam covered the distance in less than an hour, but when he checked the time, he was late anyway. He trudged up the steps, perspiration was making his shirt stick to him like Velcro. Beads of sweat ran from the bill of his cap down his shaved head and dripped off his chin. He was in no condition to sit in a classroom, but he had to, he had no choice. Judge O'Brien had made that perfectly clear. Attend the class or go to jail.

Sam found the room number he had been given and stood outside the door listening, waiting for his shirt to dry. Parched, he was wondering why a high school didn't have a drinking fountain in the hallway. When he was a kid in high school, a long time ago there were drinking fountains everywhere. Hoping his shirt would stop dripping and his breathing would return to normal, Sam hesitated to enter. The instructor, a woman who sounded young - maybe early 30's - was still going through her introductions. "My name is Kathryn," Sam heard her say "I'll be your anger management tutor and mentor for the next 20 weeks." "Tutor... mentor," Sam mumbled the words with a disgusted look. "Whatever happened to simple English? Why can't she just say she's the teacher? Is there something wrong with being a teacher now?'"

Sam peeked around the corner into the doorway. Most of the desks were empty. No hurry going in. Obviously, he wasn't the only one who was running late. "You have all been court ordered to attend this class." The lady named Kathryn continued, stating the obvious, as if Sam didn't already know that. It was the booze - it was always the booze - that made him angry. When he was sober, he was a good man. Everyone told him so. But he couldn't give up the bottle, no matter how many meetings or classes he attended. How could he? After all that had happened - the judge had ordered him to attend this stupid class or spend a year in county lock-up. Hell, a year in county jail was a death sentence for Sam. There's no booze in county jail. "I have only one rule in this class, Kathryn was telling those students who had arrived on time. Sam wondered if 'students' was still the politically correct term. Maybe we're 'pupils' ... or 'scholars' or 'subjects', he mused.

"You must attend all my classes to receive your certification - the same certification the judge will want to see. If you miss even one class, I will notify the court that day, and I think you know what will happen from there." Kathryn paused while the students ... grumbled. "Now," she said a bit louder, "let's see who we have here today. " Sam heard the rustling of papers - like Kathryn was moving sheets around in a file folder. "Carla Warfield," Kathryn called out. Sam saw a young black girl, probably early 20's - sitting in the back, raise her hand. "That's me." Carla growled, in precise diction. "Be sure to mark down that I'm here ... on time." she added, never making eye contact

"You don't have to worry about that, Miss. Warfield," Kathryn answered just as sharply. "But," she tempered her tone, "any time you - or any of you - want to verify my attendance sheet, you are welcome to do so." "Yeah, yeah," Carla mumbled, looking at the phone in her lap. "Maybeth Simmons," Kathryn called the next name. "Right over here." a slender, immaculately dressed, white woman with a seductive sounding southern accent called out. Sam leaned to his right and caught a glimpse of the very attractive woman - early 40's - long blond hair and wearing designer clothes that appeared to be made exclusively for her. She was smiling, as if she was happy to be there. Wonder what made her angry? Sam thought silently. Probably didn't get enough allowance from her filthy rich husband. "Wayne Wade," Kathryn's eyes scanning the room.

From Sam's location he could see everyone looking around. No one else in the room seemed interested "so, no Wayne Wade?" Kathryn's voice had an edge to it. "This is not a good way to begin the class." "Not good for him, you mean," Carla Warfield corrected her. "Pardon me, Miss. Warfield," Kathryn sounded flustered by Carla's comment. "Yes, it's not very good for him," Carla repeated, louder. "For the guy you just called. It's not a good way for HIM to start the class. Whatever his name is." "Oh ... um," Kathryn cleared her throat. "Of course, yes, that's what I meant. It's not a good way for Mr. Wade to start the class." Carla turned her attention back to her cell phone, then mumbled without looking up, "I don't wanna be here, but I am. Don't care if everybody else flunks out. I need to get this judge off my back." Kathryn continued, "Kevin Archer?" A young man off to the side raised two fingers up signifying he was there. Kathryn nodded in acknowledgement and proceeded.

Sam decided the fireworks inside the classroom would be more entertaining than spying on them from outside - and he needed credit for the class too - so he stepped through the doorway. "You must be Samuel Thomas." Kathryn said, glad to have a disruption in her conversation with Carla. Surprised, Sam looked up at her, his hat still in his hand. "Yeah," he muttered, "Sorry I'm late." "The judge," Kathryn explained when Sam kept staring intently at her. "He... uh.... told me you had to attend AA meetings before, so you may be tardy from time to time." Sam nodded, tacitly telling her he now understood why she knew his name and making a mental note that he had court permission to be late. "I do hope, though, Mr. Thomas," Kathryn said with more authority, "that you will make every effort to be here on time. Tardiness can be very disruptive to the class, and you could miss vital parts of the course."

"Yeah, don't wanna make you angry," a young black man stifled a laugh as he said it. "Got to keep the anger under control and it sounded like you were gettin' a little angry at old Sam there, teacher." The rest of the class laughed while Kathryn felt her face flush. "Just who might you be, young man?" Kathryn looked at the jokester, her features stern and uncompromising. "Name's Brian Cordell," he answered with a half bow. "Make sure you put your little X in the right spot. I ain't takin' this class twice!" "I hear that," Carla said, still working the buttons on her phone. "Jennifer Potter,"

Kathryn spoke loudly, ignoring Brian's comments and doing her best to regain control of the students. "Yeah here," a little, pretty girl of 19 raised her hand. "What's your story, lily white?" Kevin snickered. "White girls who wear Prada got no reason to be angry." "Mr. Archer," Kathryn chastised. "Please hold your comments about others until you're invited to share them." Kevin chuckled. "Sure thing, Mrs. Kathryn." Kathryn was clearly getting rattled, but she pressed on, calling the next person on her attendance sheet.

"Is Thurman Hampton here?" A black man slumped low in the desk, who looked to be in his late 40's, mumbled "Here." Kathryn watched Thurman for a moment. He seemed to be hiding. He refused to make eye contact with her ... or anyone else. She made a few notes beside Thurman's name, not noticing the way the rest of the class was staring at his strange behavior. When Kathryn raised her head, Thurman was barely visible above the desktop. Kathryn did not believe in premonitions; her education and training taught her that the foundation of a person's actions and feelings was a result of their environment. Yet, at that very moment, viewing the man cowering in his desk. like a frightened rabbit, a shudder ran up her spine. She could feel the hair on her neck tingle and her arms bristled. Nothing in any textbook prepared her for what she felt - foreboding ominous fear!

Chapter Eleven

Protect the ones you love

KEVIN ARCHER HAD DARTED out the door of the supermarket when he ran into his buddy Ricky. "Hey man!" Ricky Shriber giggled when he saw his friend rushing from the store. Ricky was much shorter than the 6'4" Kevin, Ricky was surrounded by a dozen cigarette butts crushed out on the sidewalk, a smoky haze hanging in the corridor. Ricky laughed again, his nervousness making his entire body jitter and contort. "Any good-lookin' chicks in there?" As he craned his neck around the door opening, scanning the females. "Come on," Kevin grabbed his shoulder and tugged him along. "You were supposed to be watching my spot - now I got to go take care of things myself, and you better hope nothing happened while you're tryin' to keep up with me."

"Oh, Kev," Ricky twisted spasmodically under Kevin's strong grip, I did watch your spot man. For real, I did. I just ... I just needed a little somethin' ... to keep me awake ... ya know?" "Shut up," Kevin's low growl silenced the little man. "This ain't some neighborhood hang out. "Sorry Kev," Ricky whined. "I ... I just ... you know man ...I need somethin' ... to help me ..." Kevin put more pressure on Ricky's shoulder and felt him wince under the pain. "What's goin' on at my house?" he asked, his face lowered, his hot breath covering Ricky. "No ... nothin', Kev." Ricky's walk was distorted, the clamp on his shoulder aching. "You gonna get me somethin'?" "You sure no one's been around ... at least while you were there?"

The anger in Kevin's voice was evident. "Ain't nobody gonna come around there," Ricky whispered. "Nobody gonna mess with Camilla again - not after what you did to...why you so worried?" "Cuz I saw him!" Kevin blurted loudly. "He tried to hide, but it was him ... I'm sure of it!" Different hair cut but it was him. "How?" Ricky mumbled, slobbering on himself. "I thought he was dead." "Apparently not," Kevin nearly yelled, shoving Ricky through the double metal doors. "I told you to watch the house, and now I see this piece of shit... if he sent someone over there ... I'm taking it out on you." "Ah, man, Kev," Ricky teared up, his voice whiny and weak. "Don't hurt me. We're buddies, right Kevin? Pals, you and me." "I can't count on you anymore, Ricky," Kevin said. "You let me down every time I try to. Just like at the house that night, you remember?"

Kevin and Ricky had left the poker game late, arriving at Camilla's house after midnight – they arrived to find Kevin's girlfriend nearly hysterical. When Kevin saw her, crumpled on the floor, her robe was bloody, and her face was stained with tears. He charged through the open door. "Sweetie!" He shouted "What happened? Are you okay!?" Kevin could see Sam Thomas, Camilla's father, nearly passed out in the recliner. He was drunk again. "Mr. Thomas!" he yelled, then pulled Camilla up to him. "What happened here? Did he…" He pointed a finger at Sam, his eyes searching the room "Where is Andre? Where is my son?" "It wasn't him," Camila said softly. She turned to look at her father "I was raped… He left out the front door…My father did nothing."

Kevin's rage was uncontrolled. "How?!" He demanded. 'Your father… He's right there…!" "He was passed out." Camilla clung to Kevin weeping. "He didn't even hear. I yelled for him to help me, but he just kept sleeping. The lights from the police vehicle lit up the front of the house and two officers approached the door. The commotion, the lights, and the loud voices finally woke Sam from his stupor. Groggily he tried to assess the room and the situation. "What'd you do?" he slurred looking at Camilla. His head unsteady. "Why are you bringing the cops around my house?" "I was raped daddy!" she cried out. Sam clenched his fists and staggered to his feet "Get out!" He screamed. "Get out of my house!" Camilla's face dropped. Her mouth fell open. "What?" "You heard me you slut!" Sam mumbled loudly through the effects of the alcohol. "Don't want a slut who brings the law around to my house! Get out!" Camilla's heart felt like it had ruptured.

"But I was raped! Here... In the house! I saw him. He has a large tattoo on his arm. It runs up to his neck... I..." "Get out!!" Sam slurred even louder, his words, barely understandable. "Tell me what happened?!" Demanded Kevin. Camilla began, "I got undressed to take a shower. Then out of nowhere appeared a guy with a knife to my throat. One hand covered my mouth, shoving me down on the bed, forcing his legs between mine. I was terrified. Thinking this man could kill me and no one would know what happened. At that moment I prayed asking God is this really happening to me? Am I about to be raped??' He laid the knife on the bed, then used one hand to cover my mouth and used his other hand, and put one finger to his mouth, puckering his lips, telling me to be quiet. "If you scream, I'll kill you." He said, with such force as he moved his hand from my mouth to quickly unfasten his pants. I felt helpless... helpless and alone.

My body was tense when he forced himself inside of me so hard, I literally thought my insides were going to rupture. As tears streamed down my face, he penetrated me. It felt like a million stickpins sticking me all at once. He laid his torso on my breast and continued moving up and down. I kept my fists balled up as tight as I could just staring at the white ceiling above as I laid there, smelling his sweat and musk. In fact, I can still smell him hovering over me. I felt so ashamed because I started to get wet. 'How could this be a thought! I hate this guy!!' I started to fight back to resist him. Then he started choking me, piercing the knife into my side, he made a small incision. Then I heard him moan. I was disgusted! Right before I felt him cum inside of me. I was overwhelmed. His semen raced through my body like poison."

Camilla continued "It seemed to last forever, but really it only lasted three or four minutes, which was the worst minutes of my life. He pulled himself out of me. He stood up and fastened his pants. He told me to turn my head as he left the room. I reached for a pillow or anything I could get my hands on to wipe his smelly sweat off my breast, and in between my legs. I was petrified, but relieved it was over ... I grew numb. Wondering to myself what did I do to deserve this? Did God in the most dramatic moment of my life, stop loving me? Then the shame and resentment began to set in. I started crying. I was all alone for a moment not knowing what to do next. I got up off the bed and ran to my father's room. I felt the warm fluid of his semen drip down my legs as I tried to awaken my father." "Where's Andre?" Kevin asked again. "In his crib," she motioned. Kevin left the room to check on his son. He returned moments later with the sleeping toddler held tightly in his arms.

"You're staying with me," he told her, nearly shoving her out the door. The waiting policeman quickly surrounded them. After hearing their story and documenting the allegation, Camilla and Kevin were escorted to the station where Camilla looked through piles of mug shot books. "He's not here," she sighed, exhausted. "He's not in your books." "Tomorrow, we'll need you to meet with a sketch artist," one of the officers said. "Maybe we'll get lucky, and someone will recognize him." "I'll recognize him," she assured them. "I'll never forget that tattoo ... those eyes, that breath." "And I'll be looking for that tattoo myself," Kevin hissed, his anger seething through his entire body.

One of the policemen eyed him carefully. "You best just leave the police work to us son," he warned. "This man is dangerous ... and anything you do to him will be a crime. You don't want to go to jail, do you?" Kevin returned the stare. "I don't want this creep to get away with what he did." "Then leave him to us," the officer relaxed a bit after the second warning. "We'll do our job. We'll find this guy."

Kevin didn't know how to control his anger, so he lashed out at any and every one that looked or stared at him improperly. Or... what he thought to be improperly. He wanted to impose pain on the world... thinking that would release the pain in his heart. His rampage landed him in front of judge O'Brien. Kevin, like the rest of the class, was given the option of going to jail or participate in the anger management class as an alternative sentence. Kevin always wondered what jail would be like. He had heard so many stories, good and bad. Because of his curiosity he considered taking the jail sentence. But doing that would leave Camilla and Andre unprotected. He was stuck taking the class.

Two weeks later, after repeated calls to the police station, and receiving the same answer each time. "Nothing new Mr. Archer." Kevin walked into an auto body shop several blocks from where Camilla lived with her father. Peeling off a hundred dollar bill from a thick wad , he explained what he wanted. Then, with an attitude, pressed the money into the greasy man's outstretched palm. For several long seconds their eyes bore into each other. Kevin didn't blink. His face was stone - anger etched in every feature. "OK youngster," the body man finally nodded. "I know dude and that tattoo. I don't have an address, but I know where he stay." "Where?" Kevin demanded. The man pocketed the money, then told him. Kevin and Ricky knew the area - probably had seen the man many times. They arrived at the house under the cover of night - sneaking stealthily, communicating with hand signals. Ricky went to the front door - his assignment was to lure the man to the front of the house so Kevin could slide in the back door, trapping the rapist in his own home.

There was no doubt they had the right guy, the tattoo - visible even in the dark, unlit house – was exactly as Camilla described it, his limp just as she said, matched what she saw when the man hobbled away. It was him - it was the guy who had raped Camilla. Ten minutes later, after the most pathetic pleading and whimpering Kevin had ever seen, he and Ricky walked out of the house. The man they left behind - the one beaten and bloody with a broken baseball bat jammed viciously into his rectum - could easily identify them if he wanted. "You make me sick." Kevin said before leaving the barely conscious man. Blood was oozing from his lips and cuts on his face - and it was streaming from his ferociously violated anus. Bruises and welts were already appearing on his torso. "Now you know what it feels like to be raped!" Kevin spat on the man again, then slammed the door behind him.

The images would haunt most men. They haunted Ricky but Kevin was unaffected. Kevin's background - especially his youth - had been filled with violence and anger even more atrocious than what he just done to the man. Kevin had come to believe that anger and violence was the solution to every situation and being the biggest, toughest, and the meanest was the key to staying alive at the end of the day. It was the language he knew best. "So ... so you think dude is still .... alive?" Ricky sputtered as he talked, the twitching increasing in severity. "After what you did to him that night?"

Chapter Twelve

Disguising your fears

"HEY SWEET BABY," WAYNE Wade craned his neck in the small desk to watch Carla Warfield as she entered the classroom, "I know some real anger management therapy you and I could perform together." Carla, 19 years old and easily fitting into the category of 'gorgeous', smirked nastily at the ogling boy. "Put it away little man." she snarled. "I don't do white boys." Wayne assumed she was just playing hard-to-get.

Carla seemed to have an edgy attitude that he found appealing. The 'fall-all-over' white girls he had been with were starting to turn him off. He wanted a challenge. "I guess that means you want me then." Wayne leaned sideways to block Carla's path down the aisle "Because I ain't been a boy since I was in diapers ... and even then, I'm not sure." "Big talk," Carla dressed him down with her eyes, "for such a little fellow."

Sensitive about his slight stature, Wayne struck back. "Got a body like a model and a tongue like a biatch." he said. Carla slammed her purse on the desk beside her. "What did he just call me?" Without making eye contact with anyone, she scanned the room. "What did this little punk just call me?" Wayne, grinning again, reached up for Carla's arm. Before he could grab it, Brian leaped from his desk and stood between them. A young muscular black guy with steely eyes and a prominent jawline, Brian towered over the smaller man still seated in the desk. "You owe the lady an apology." he growled at Wayne. "Then I guess this chick will never be broke," Wayne smart- mouthed back, "because she'll always have that uncollected debt on her books." "I said apologize to the lady," Brian clenched his fists as if he were going to punch Wayne.

Wayne stood up – he was several inches shorter than Brian - but lacking no courage. "You best give me 50 feet homie," he stood toe to toe with the bigger man, "You think you know anger, you ain't seen nothin' yet." Brian leaned forward just as Carla shoved him, nearly toppling him onto Wayne, "You supposed to be some kind of black superhero?" she was just as nasty to him as she was to Wayne. "Just so you know ... and don't misunderstand, I don't do buffed up macho brothers either. I fight my own battles and neither of you are worth fighting for." She flopped into her desk and ignored them. Wayne and Brian continued glaring at each other until Wayne broke into a huge grin, then a laugh. Offended, Brian turned and glared at Carla. She jerked in her seat, moving the desk farther away from him. "Ah, I see you're not into dark meat either," Brian taunted her. "Or maybe you don't like men at all, is that it?" "When I see a man, I'll let you know," she snapped.

Kathryn, who had cautiously entered the room in the middle of the exchange, rang a small bell she had on the desk, her heartbeat racing as she tried to calm the class. "Please ... please take your seats," she squeaked. "It's time to start. Sit down all of you." She grabbed the attendance sheet from her folder, then made a quick glance at the students. "I see you're here on time today, Mr. Wade," she began, addressing him personally in an attempt to distract him from the confrontation and diffuse it. Wayne looked her way. "Yeah, thought I better please the judge. Keep him happy, you know?" "He ain't no Priest," Brian said as he was taking his seat. Wayne erupted. "What the hell is that supposed to mean?!" He shouted shoving the front of Brian's desk. Surprised, Brian jerked backwards. "Hey, nothin' man," he said "just that the judge is a man ... like us ... "

He shot a glance at Carla. "At least some of us are men. He - the judge - he ain't no saint .. he ain't no Priest ... he's just a man." Wayne huffed a few more times, finally concluding Brian did not know about Father Murphy then he calmed himself and slowly eased back to his desk. Kathryn's mind was filled with images of Wayne and Father Murphy. Her anxiety skyrocketed as she recalled Doctor Stephenson reading from the boy's file. Putting a face - a living person - to the abuse made her nauseous.

Steadying herself with both hands anchored to the podium in a death grip, she slowed her breathing and resumed her roll call. "Is Sam present?" The tactic worked. Every class member turned their heads looking at Sam. "Judge not gonna like that," Jennifer said, then just as swiftly she turned her attention back to her phone. "Just make sure you mark down my name." Brian reminded her sitting now, his attention no longer on Wayne. "I hear that," Carla snapped her fingers above her head. "And mines too."

Chapter Thirteen

Unprepared

"How's your anger management tutor handling the job?" Dr. Fuquan asked as he and Dr. Stephenson nursed their beers at the quiet tavern halfway between their two offices. Clay Stephenson shrugged. "I don't hear a lot and I'm so busy I can't get over there," he confessed. "You ever taught anger management?" James sipped his beer, remembering the anger that once controlled every aspect of his life. "I counseled people, but never taught a class.? he said soberly. Stephenson smoothed down his moustache with his thumb and finger. "The girl knows everything she has ever been taught. She can practically quote a textbook." "I hear a – but ..." Dr. Fuquan urged him to continue.

Clay nodded. "But, when I do see her," he looked off towards the bar, "she seems different. I mean ... maybe she's just rushing around trying to do too much with this added class and all. But she's ... frazzled. Is that a good word?" Fuquan smiled.

"It's in my vocabulary," he said. "Maybe it's too much for her. There's a lot of stress being around individuals who harbor so much venom ... hey what am I doing? You're the expert here. What do you think is going on?" Stephenson sat his glass on the round table and cocked his head sideways. "It's just a feeling, she's never said anything, but I feel like she's coming undone."

"And good doctor," James Fuquan tried to keep the conversation light and casual, "why haven't you asked her?" Stephenson laughed and took a long draw from the stein. "These are angry people. They're not killers. I thought it would be an easy class to teach. One she could handle. I guess I can't understand her struggles." James Fuquan squeezed his lips taut. Flashes of his own past, a past only Clay Stephenson knew. "You ever been abused?" he asked his friend, a dark edge to his voice. "Ever been sexually abused .. or set up ... or abused by your friends in any way?" "You mean ... not just sexually?" "I mean abused," Fuquan raised his voice for the first time in years. The anger from days long buried, days he thought were dead and behind him - was suddenly controlling him again.

"No, James." Stephenson clutched his beer with both hands as he confessed his lack of understanding. "I've never been abused at least nothing like you have." "And nothing like any of those in that class," Dr. Fuquan quickly reminded him.

"Hell, the girl leading the class is just another victim like the one's she's trying to help. I imagine every emotion - even the tiniest flare up in the class - brings back her own haunting memories." Dr. Stephenson contritely tried to reduce the agitation his colleague was feeling, "I haven't done all I could to prepare this girl. I know that now. I thought this would be the ideal ice breaker for her - a group who either finishes the class or goes to prison. I guess I assumed they'd want to avoid jail time." "They do," Dr. Fuquan calmed himself. "I'm sorry Clay. I didn't mean to flare up. The people in that class do want to avoid jail time ... believe me."

Dr. Fuquan continued "Every smoker wants to quit smoking, every alcoholic wants to quit the drinking. Drug addicts tell themselves daily that they'll quit tomorrow. And round and round again, the beat goes on. Anger is no different. It's an addiction. I believe the brain sends signals when a person vents his anger on someone else much like it does when a fat person eats a donut. It's a temporary fix - a momentary high. Only anger is worse. Anger gives you power - creates fear. Later the obese man regrets eating the donut, but the angry man can actually gain power by demonstrating his angry side, and he feels justified. Then his mind tells him that's the only way to get what he wants."

Dr. Stephenson was nodding. Nothing his friend was saying was new to him. His problem was experience. Dr. Stephenson had grown up in the upper-class suburbs, the privileged son of prominent parents. Anger, any emotion, really was unacceptable in his home. As good as he was at his profession, he never had been able to empathize with his patients. Losing control of your emotions was beyond his field of experience and remained an aberration in an otherwise ideal life. "What can I do to help her?" Dr. Stephenson asked, submitting to his colleague, who had a lifetime of experience behind him. "It's what can WE do Clay?"

James Fuquan looked concerned. "He scratched his temple and ran his hand over his head. Doctor Stephenson was silent, curiously waiting at the mercy of his fellow psychologist. "Why don't you call her tomorrow. It's Thursday, last day of class this week. We need to monitor her closer. James, can you make an appointment to visit her on Friday. Let's see how she feels. It's been 3 weeks now, enough time to get a report." Stephenson nodded. "I'll make the call, and Fuquan ... thank you." Dr. Fuquan reached across the small table and patted Clay shoulder. "Don't thank me yet." he said. "If I'm right, and I hope I'm not, she could lose it in this class. If she does ... well... " His voice trailed off and his gaze went blank. "Well, what?" Dr. Stephenson waited anxiously. James

Fuquan returned his focus to the man across from him. "If she loses it, these people will be lost forever, and some may act out in anger." Stephenson swallowed hard: "You're talking emotionally, right not physically." Dr. Fuquan stared at him a long moment, "I'm talking both."

Chapter Fourteen

Left to pick up the pieces

MAYBETH SIMMONS PUSHED OPEN the door to the empty house. No one was there but the ghosts. Thoughts of her precious little girl Amber, lying in that box beneath the ground ... the sound of the dirt slapping on the coffin lid as the workers filled the grave ... haunted her from within the walls of her house and within the walls of her mind. The laughter and happy times that once echoed through this house now mocked her, sinking her heart into despair. She was alone - and every moment inside her own tormented mind ... each second in her own house - brought back memories that would never return. The photographs on the walls - a family, smiling, having fun, vacationing together ... each one a painful reminder of all that she had lost.

In the darkness she was sure she could see Amber. Was her daughter there standing, waiting for her to rush to her and embrace her? "Is that you, honey?" she called out. "Amber ... Ashley are you girls here? Are you waiting for Mommy?" Why were they standing there ... why weren't they running to her with their arms outstretched ... like so many times before? No - she could see now - it was an illusion ... they were gone, both of them. Amber was dead. Ashley was in foster care. Their father, her husband was incarcerated.

The day it all turned around from a cheerful, successful family to this devastation replayed through her mind like a horror movie on a continuous loop. "One day," she lied to herself, knowing there were signs - many of them - and she should have seen them ... should have realized what was happening. She should have protected her little girl - from the monster that lived with them. Maybeth turned on the light ... Amber wasn't there, of course, and neither was Ashley. Maybeth sank into the carpet, crumpled on the floor, the horrible video replaying again ... so real ... so torturing. She was sure she could hear their voices ... just like before ...

"I don't want any breakfast," Amber grumbled, her vacant eyes staring at her mother. "But you're getting so skinny sweetheart. You need to eat." "I need a lot more than that." Amber mumbled. "But what the hell do you care?" "Amber!"

Maybeth scolded, "You know I don't approve of that kind of language. I swear I don't know what is going on with you anymore. You're a different girl." Her voice remained accusatory, her eyes narrowing in anger. "The attitude, the way you dress, all that makeup, and now the language!" "I gotta go to school." Amber slammed her chair backwards and marched out the door, slamming it behind her.

Maybeth clutched the dish towel to her breasts, watching Amber disappear around the hedges. "Is Amber mad, Mommy?" 4-year-old Ashley asked, slurping her cereal milk from the bowl. Maybeth sighed. "She's 16," she nearly whispered, as if that explained everything. "I'm gonna be nice to you when I'm 16 mommy!" Ashley said, trying to lick the milk off her chin. "I love you, Mommy." "And I love you, pumpkin." Maybeth wiped a tear from her eye then bent and kissed her daughter's forehead.

Leon Simmons refused to discuss their daughter's deviance, waving his arm at Maybeth, then headed for the den. "She's just a teenager," he said over his shoulder. "She'll outgrow whatever it is that's bothering her. I've had a long day. The council is planning next year's budget. I don't have time for...." "No time for your daughter?" Maybeth challenged. "No time for your family?" Leon stopped, turned and looped an arm around his wife. "You know everything I do is for you and the kids," he told her, pulling her into him. "I would never neglect my children. You have to know that, after all I've done for them." Maybeth nodded and Leon vanished into the den. "Maybe you never neglect your children," Maybeth moaned aloud when the door to the den closed her out, "but what about me?" She tried to remember the last time they made love ... it's been too long ... she couldn't recall ... there was not even an interest on his part.

Sleep wouldn't come that night for Maybeth. Her mind was filled with conflicting thoughts. She was hoping Leon would want her tonight. She leaned on him and snuggled close. But he was already asleep, his rhythmic breathing shutting her out once again. It was like he had a switch, as soon as his head hit the pillow he was snoring. Usually, Maybeth would doze off to sleep too. The confrontation with Amber however, kept running through her mind. She tried to mentally recite poetry ... counted backwards from 100... tense and relax each part of her body.... nothing worked. All she could see was Amber's blank stare.

It was well past midnight. Maybeth had been lying awake for a couple of hours when she felt Leon stir. Maybeth got excited. Maybe, her heart raced, just maybe he was desiring her after all! She had tried many times, but it was hopeless. He was asleep each time. She held her breath, hoping, anticipating. Slowly, methodically, like each movement was a delicate chore, Leon slid to the edge of the bed and gently swung his feet off. In a measured calculated maneuver, he rose to his feet. Leon stealthily crossed the room in the darkness. Softly he eased open the door and left the bedroom. She could only wonder what he was doing, where he was going.

He made his descent down the hallway as quickly as he could to Amber's room. Seven-year-old Amber was lying in bed fast asleep. Leon caressed her little body, waking her up. "Amber, sweetie, wake up." Groggily amber responded. "Hello daddy, I'm sleepy." She slowly moved her body to attention, Leon whispered, "Daddy wants to play a game with you Amber." "Do you want me to get Mommy?" "No, this is just a game for me and you. Do you want to play with daddy?" Amber replied ecstatically "Yes!" "OK good." Leon said "we're going to play a game of tickle. You have to lay on your back and close your eyes. I'm going to tickle you, but you can't laugh out loud, OK?" Amber was excited, now wide awake and ready to play. She was smiling from ear to ear. Leon spoke softly "OK babe, lay down and close your eyes. As he began to tickle her under her torso, she wiggled her body and began to laugh, rising up looking face-to-face with her daddy. Leon stopped tickling.

"OK, let's do this again." This time he kneeled on the floor. He began pulling her little body to the edge of the bed, "Amber, daddy's going to take your undies off OK baby?" Amber was confused, "But why daddy?" she asked, "I like my underwear on." Leon replied, "Because this is how we play the special game OK?" Confused, Amber agreed "OK daddy." As he removed her a little flower adorned underwear he said, "OK babe now shut your eyes. Daddy is going to tickle you." Spreading her legs apart Leon began kissing and licking her private parts... After several minutes had passed, he put her undies back on and said, "OK baby, you have to remember. This is our little secret. You cannot tell anyone OK? Not even mommy." "OK daddy," she said, with her head down, tears rolling down her cheeks.

"Why are you crying baby?" Amber replied "Because," Amber paused and then said, "I don't know." Leon hugged her tight and said "Daddy loves you. Don't cry babe. Tomorrow daddy will take you to get ice cream. OK?" quietly Amber replied, "OK daddy." Leon reminded her "You have to promise me you won't tell anyone about our little game OK, now you have to stop crying." He started to tickle her again, "Now go back to sleep, OK? Daddy loves you." Amber replied, "I love you too daddy." just before the door closed. This was the first of many times Amber was molested at the hands of her father Leon. Thirty minutes later he returned to his bedroom. This time Leon immediately went to the bathroom to brush his teeth, finally cautiously coaxing his body gingerly, back into the bed beside his wife. Maybeth laid rigidly still, wideawake. In less than a minute, Leon breathing evenly again. The breath of a content man fast asleep.

The next morning, life changed as they all knew it. Amber seemed different...quiet. Usually, Amber was the most talkative and bouncy child Maybeth had ever seen. Now, she would just stare at her plate and move around the food. Her smile slowly faded over the next several years. Things that she once enjoyed...she now discarded. Amber was being disruptive in school. At night Amber would cry and beg her mother to sleep in her bed with her. Maybeth was growing frustrated with her child's growing behavior problem. Keeping this secret was slowly taking away the sweet, bubbly, precocious little girl and replacing her with a scared and withdrawn victim. Amber couldn't tell anyone. The guilt was eating her up inside, devouring her innocence. She knew it was bad. None of her friend's played 'secret games'. She knew, if someone said it's a secret, it was bad. Keeping secrets was bad. The abuse continued and Maybeth failed to put the pieces together to solve the puzzle.

Chapter Fifteen

Not color blind

MAYBETH WAS LIKE A zombie, completely exhausted from another sleepless night, Maybeth ushered Amber out of the door the next morning, then collapsed on the living room sofa while Ashley played around her. Stirring herself awake around noon, her first thoughts were of Amber. Refreshed from her nap, Maybeth's irritation from her daughter's behavior returned. A quick lunch for Ashley and then MayBeth climbed the stairs to Amber's bedroom. Maybe there was a clue there that could explain why her daughter was acting so rebellious. Maybe there was something that would convince her that her daughter was just going through a phase, and that she was not suffering from the same secret Maybeth kept hidden for all those years.

Maybeth watched Amber pick at dinner, her head down, her long, bangs dyed jet black were covering her face. Discord was not what Maybeth wanted: neither was conflict. She saw no way to avoid it though, not after what she had found in Amber's room, Leon was slicing his steak while glancing at a stack of papers at his elbow. It's now or never Maybeth thought. "Amber!" she blurted out a bit too loudly, her nerves making her shake. Her startled daughter snapped her head up. "What's this?" Maybeth asked shoving a photograph across the table. Amber took a casual peek, then her eyes popped open, her breathing sped up. "You're going through my room now?" she hollered, slapping her palm on the table. "What is this place a prison?"

Leon grabbed the photo. "Let me see that?" "She's kissing a colored boy." Maybeth huffed. "After all we have taught her. And there's another one up there ... hidden under her pillow." Leon erupted. "I want this stopped, young lady! I want this to end right now, you hear me? Don't you ever see this colored boy again!" His face was red, and his veins were protruding his neck. Amber jumped to her feet, her food spilling across the table and onto the floor, then she ran from the room. "I can't believe this," Leon poked a finger at Maybeth, his other hand shaking the photograph. "Can't you control your own daughter? Do I have to do everything around here?" Maybeth could barely breathe. "You're blaming me?" "I can't be here all day," Leon shouted. "I have to work. Someone has to finance your spending habits."

He shook his head in disgust. "How could you let this happen?" Tears poured from Maybeth's eyes, and she too ran from the room. Maybeth was in the laundry room the next day when she heard Amber stomp up the stairs after school. The morning had been a nightmare. Amber refused breakfast and rushed out of the house in an angry fit. "I'll make up with her tonight." Maybeth told herself several times throughout the day. Her own adolescence was not that far in the past. She could remember clearly the trauma of raging hormones and the drama of trying to cope with a developing body. "Maybe Leon is right." she reasoned. "Maybe I need to be more of a mother to her ... spend more time with her. Tonight, I'll make it up to her. We'll talk - like we used to - and plan something ... a girl's night out. ... or a trip to the salon." Just the thought of reconciliation with Amber cheered up her day.

"Amber, sweetie," she called from outside her door. "Can I come in? Just to talk?" "It ain't locked," came a snarling response from inside the room. "I'm sure the prison guard has a key anyway." 'I tried' Maybeth thought. She clenched her jaw and grabbed Amber's cheeks, forcing her to look up. "What is wrong with you?" she snapped. "What happened to you?" Amber twisted her face out of Maybeth's grip. "You want to know what's wrong with me? You really want to know?" She was yelling, as fury darted from her eyes. "I'll tell you ... Mommy!" She mockingly sneered. "I'm sick of having my own father come into my room at night and force me to have sex with him!! My father has been forcing me to have sex with him for the past 9 years - he's been abusing me - right under your nose - and you didn't do a thing about it. You must find him disgusting too because he has wants to have sex with me - his daughter!"

Maybeth's mouth gaped open like a broken gate. Without thinking, her hand swept up and slashed across Amber's face, slapping her - leaving a red handprint on her cheek. "Don't you ever say that!" she screamed, stunned, shocked. "Don't you ever speak that way about your father. You understand Me?" Amber timidly touched her cheek, tears gushing from her eyes and cascading down her face. For a moment they stared at each other - both too stunned to speak. Then Amber snatched up her backpack and ran from the room. Maybeth heard the front door slam shut.

Chapter Sixteen

A painful reminder

LIKE SYRUP FLOWING FROM a bottle - or blood oozing from a wound - Maybeth slithered uncomfortably from the sofa, her body wilting on the floor in a turmoil of pain tears and grief. How could this have happened? Her beautiful family! Her perfect life! Her daughter her pride and joy ... her own husband! She sobbed. Unlike the soaking tears she had shed so many times recently, this came from deep within her - a wracking excruciating wailing - the howling of a damned soul. Maybeth slammed her hands over her ears, but the sound of Amber's voice still reverberated through her "My father has been forcing me to have sex with him ... for the past 9 years!" She clamped her eyelids tight together, but it could not take away the image of what she saw that day - the day Ashley found the letter.

"I found a letter from Amber, Mommy," Maybeth heard Ashley's voice tell her. "Will you read it to me?" Smiling, Maybeth took the neatly folded paper. She opened it and read the words that had splintered her life: "I don't want to live this way any longer. I can't live this way. Sorry I wasn't good enough for your love. At least now I won't be a burden to you any longer. It's over now - finally. My life never did matter. But now I'm at peace." Panic seized Maybeth. "Ashley," She grabbed the young girl by the arm. "Where did you get this? Where?!" she demanded.

Frightened, Ashley pointed to the stairs. "In Amber's room," she stammered, almost crying. "I was looking for," Maybeth was running up the stairs. "Amber! " She shouted. "Amber honey, Amber, where are you?" A dreaded sickness filled her stomach, her entire body heaving with an unknown fear. "Amber! " Maybeth screamed again, tearing open her daughter's door. The room was just as it had been earlier. Nothing out of place - and no Amber. Maybeth screamed again, rushing from the bedroom to the bathroom, pulling back the shower curtain. "Amber!" she hollered, the cry of a mother who'd lost her cub. "I can help you find her," Ashley volunteered, her large blue eyes following her mother. When Maybeth rushed to the guest room, Ashley slipped away. Moments later Ashley called out, "I found her, Mommy." Ashley began tugging on Maybeth's sleeve. "I found Amber." "Where?" Maybeth was shaking. "Where is she?" "In the closet. In her room." "The closet?" Maybeth repeated, then darted down the hall to Amber's room again.

When she tore open the closet door, Maybeth witnessed the most horrific scene any mother can imagine. The small hassock was over- turned on the floor, just below Amber's dangling feet, her neck stretched from the cord binding it. "NO!" Maybeth wailed so loudly Ashley was startled and ran out of the room. Maybeth grabbed Amber's legs, holding her up - shaking, crying, praying. She managed to pull down the rod, spilling clothes, purses and stuffed animals. Amber's eyes were bulging - wide open in a vacant stare - blood oozing from the corners. Her face was purple. "No! No! No!" Maybeth screamed again. "Please, no, baby, oh my Amber, no, please don't do this, baby, please!" The next few hours were a blur. She must have called 9-1-1 because an ambulance arrived in minutes. Amber' s body was taken away. Leon was contacted. He rushed home, the family doctor. was summoned. He had no choice but to sedate the hysterical mother. The powerful drug Maybeth received was the only thing that could block out the horrible scene ... and that was temporary.

The ringing telephone woke Maybeth the next morning - a call that changed her life once again. "My name is Grayson Mitchell," the dignified sounding man identified himself. "I'm the County Coroner." Maybeth managed a muffled acknowledgement. "I hate to bother you, Mrs. Simmons, at such a terrible time," the coroner spoke softly. "But something has come up in the autopsy of your daughter." Maybeth felt her body spasms begin anew. It was true .. it wasn't a nightmare. Her baby was gone. Amber was dead. And now some man - this Coroner - was carving up her body like it was a science project. "What is it?" Maybeth weakly asked, barely interested. "Your daughter," Grayson Mitchell said, "she was pregnant." Maybeth was suddenly very interested.

Chapter Seventeen

Misplaced anger

IT WAS NOW MAKING sense. "There has to be something here," Maybeth mumbled to herself as she tore through every drawer and storage bin in Amber's room. "I'll find that kid. I can't believe she had sex with a black boy. He must have gotten her pregnant and dumped her. That's why she did that to herself!" Papers were scattered everywhere. The room looked like the aftermath of a tornado. Maybeth sat on the floor, tears fell from her eyes, even when she didn't think she had any tears left. Then, through the blur, she spotted it - Amber's laptop - hidden under the bed beneath several shoe boxes. Maybeth leaped like a hungry puma, yanking the device from its seclusion. With a hasty urgency, she flipped open the lid and typed in the password. "Sure, glad we made that a requirement to having a computer." she sighed, recalling the night at Best Buy when they purchased the system, insisting they have a copy of her password.

The computer booted up. Maybeth searched the icons and clicked on the address book. "How will I know who he is?" she wondered. "Unless YES!" She pumped her fist. Amber had included a photo beside each name in her book. The boy's face was on the second page. "Mark Harcrow," Maybeth pronounced the name like she was reading a poisonous recipe. Grabbing a pen, she wrote the name and address on her hand, then opened the file ... and hit jackpot. Dozens more pictures popped up and, in one particular shot, Mark was wearing a Lowe's Hardware smock over his shirt. The nametag pinned to it, with the Lowe's logo, said, "HI, MY NAME IS Mark." "So it is," Maybeth's guttural growl sounded feral. "Time to go to Lowe's," she said.

Assuming the boy went to Amber's school, Maybeth deduced he worked at the Lowe's just a mile from their house. She stalked into the building - a warrior on the hunt. She searched the aisles, then spotted Mark at the checkout. Her heart was pounding, her breathing erratic. She wanted to leap at him - to rip him - shred him - make him pay in pain the way she was suffering. Indiscriminately, Maybeth loaded a shopping cart with items near her, then pushed the cart to Mark's register line. Her eyes were flaring rage as she waited for him to finish with the customer ahead of her.

"Good afternoon, Ma'am." Mark greeted her. "Did you find everything you ... " Maybeth snapped, her self-control completely gone. She began throwing the items from the cart, hitting him with each toss. She was screaming, yelling, calling him names. The surprised boy huddled in the corner of the checkout booth, covering himself with his arms, trying to avoid the flying objects. Quickly, several Lowe's employees rushed to the booth and took hold of Maybeth, pulling her away from the cart and clutching her tight. "Ma'am!" one of the supervisors was saying, "Ma'am, hold on, wait, please settle down. Let's see what this is all about. Don't keep fighting me Ma'am!" Two Lowe's employees clung to Maybeth while she swung her arms wildly, fighting like a feral lion. "You son-of-a-bitch," she screamed. "You made my daughter kill herself." Her long fingernails were flashing and clawing, trying to get at Mark.

Maybeth was still not yet settled when the police arrived. She was handcuffed while officers took statements from employees and customers who had witnessed the scene. "He got my daughter pregnant," Maybeth yelled, her sobbing, quivering voice carrying through the store. "She was only a child. He needs to be arrested, not me!" "NO!" Mark shook his head, his voice pleading. "That's not true. We never ... never had not even once." "Liar!" Maybeth screamed. "I spoke to the coroner. She, was pregnant when she died." "It was not mine," Mark shouted back. "I swear it's not!" "We'll sort this out," the officer promised them both. "We'll get DNA tests and then we'll know if he was the father." He was looking at Maybeth. "But right now, Ma'am you're going to have to go downtown with us, to headquarters. You are being charged with aggravated assault."

Maybeth didn't care. Nothing mattered any more. Nothing was worth living for. "Wait!" she screeched, planting her feet solidly, knowing there was something precious she still cared for. "My baby, my daughter Ashley. She's in the car." The policeman stared at her. "You left your child in the car!" His look was one of incredulity. He quickly told a female officer to take the child to CPS. "She's an unfit mother right now," the arresting officer said. "That is one thing we do know for sure." He stuffed Maybeth, hysterical and weeping, into the backseat of the cruiser. "At least we can save one of her children."

Chapter Eighteen

Consequences

"WE'RE GOING TO LET you go to your daughter's funeral," Judge O'Brien told Maybeth from the bench. "Unescorted. You have posted bail, so you are free to go, but let me remind you that you are still under the custody of the court, charged with a felony. Any further outburst and I'll be forced to return you to a cell until trial. Am I clear on that, Mrs. Simmons?" Maybeth was contrite. "Yes, sir," she politely answered, looking thin and gaunt in the baggy orange jumpsuit.

During her time in jail, she had stayed awake - afraid to sleep. Afraid she would wake up to an even greater nightmare. Though nothing could possibly compare to finding Amber's body hanging in the closet. There were ghosts ... dreams from her past that were again rising to the surface. Her mind ached from the extensive effort to keep them out, but to no avail. Her lawyer had told her that Judge O'Brien was considering her for a new program - attendance at a series of anger management classes - in lieu of prison time. If he offered, she had decided she would accept it with the hope that the class might be a mental diversion - one that would help her rebury her past.

"Mrs. Simmons!" Judge O'Brien's voice was loud, and he whacked his gavel twice on the bench, bringing her back to the present. "Are you okay, Mrs. Simmons?" he asked when Maybeth snapped her head to look up at him. "Yes." she stammered, "Uh ... yes, Your Honor ... Judge." While the Bailiff grinned, Judge O'Brien said, "I asked if you had any questions about the conditions of your release?" "No," Maybeth shook her head. "I'm fine. Fine with them ... and I won't cause any trouble. I promise." Taking off the ugly jumpsuit felt like a new birth to Maybeth. Each step, each halting, heavy, plodding step from the limo to the looming hole where Amber would be laid to rest, made her wish it was her body in the box and not her little girls.

A constant stream of memories flooded her mind. Amber was running through the lawn sprinkler on a hot summer day .. standing so proud and tall in her kindergarten graduation picture ... when they were shopping together and laughing and sharing a pizza in the mall. Words were said by the pastor, but all Maybeth heard was the sound of the dirt falling like exploding bombs on the coffin lid after it was lowered into the ground -. covering her child ... sealing her away forever. It was a detective who finally looped his arm around Maybeth's shoulder and led her from the gravesite. Leon was already in the limo. Maybeth looked at her husband, sitting alone in the large automobile. Was he seething? She knew his expressions so well. He looked angry. Was he still blaming her? Had her arrest so embarrassed him that he was now holding a grudge?

"Mrs. Simmons," the Detective said softly as they walked away from the cemetery workers. "The DNA report came back." Maybeth cocked her head, wondering why he was sharing this information with her now. As soon as it was confirmed that Mark was the father, she would feel the rage return. "Mark Harcrow is not the father," the Detective nearly whispered. "He is not a match for the fetus your daughter was carrying." Maybeth couldn't speak. How could that be? Had Amber been sexually active with more than one partner? At her age? Was Mark correct when he adamantly denied ever having any sexual relations with Amber?

Then it hit her. If Mark wasn't the father, her memory re-played Amber's accusation - that Leon had been raping her. The thought had been so repugnant ... so repulsive that May-beth had not even considered it a possibility. She gasped and slammed her hand over her mouth. Could Leon ... Oh No!

"Please," she muttered. "That would be more than I could take ... more than I could bear." "I'm sorry," the Detective leaned his ear down closer towards her. "I couldn't hear what you said." Breathing fast and hard, Maybeth looked up at the officer with huge, frightened eyes. "Can you run a DNA check ... if I get you a sample of someone." The Detective wrinkled his forehead. "A test .... on you?" "NO! " Maybeth shook her head. "On my husband."

The Detective pulled up, clutching Maybeth by the shoulders. "If," he paused, flustered, "if ... your husband ... if it is a match." He peered at the limo where Leon continued to wait in the backseat "If it is positive - he will be arrested for child molestation and any number of other ... very serious crimes." "I know." Maybeth whispered. "But I have to know." Slowly, almost cautiously, the Detective nodded his head. "I will see that the test is run." Maybeth thanked him, though she was more frightened now than she ever had been in her life. If Leon was the father if it was true ... her life would end as she now knew it ... and it would end in a very dramatic, horrible way.

Five days later the same Detective, accompanied by his partner, rang the doorbell at the Simmons' home. The items Maybeth had given him - some hair, a coffee cup Leon had used, and his pipe - had all been tested. The results were more than conclusive ... they were absolute. "Leon Simmons?" the Detective asked, his voice deep and very serious, when Leon answered the door. Leon smiled. "You know who I am Detective Hallister. What do you want? And why are you coming to my house?" Detective Hallister removed the handcuffs from his belt. "You are under arrest, sir, please come with us peacefully." A stunned Leon was quickly subdued.

The moment he tried to resist, the officers forced him swiftly to the police car and jammed him into the cruiser. Maybeth watched from the front room window, tears flowing like opened levees. Her suspicions had been confirmed ... her beautiful life ... her stature in the community ... her reputation ... had all been a lie - a horrible, shameful, disgusting, filthy lie. Maybe she deserved this, she thought. Maybe this was merited ... after what she had done ... so long ago.

Chapter Nineteen

Trust is earned

THE WHISKY BOTTLE STARED back at him from the coffee table daring him ... calling for him. Sam Thomas tried to look away - tried to avoid the lure of the smooth, enticing brown liquid. He could feel his tongue going between his teeth and his lips - then darting out of his mouth in ejaculating spurts as if it could snatch the bottle like a frog catches flies, and pull it in to him. His hands were jittery, his palms were sweaty, and, worst of all, he knew that the discomfort he was feeling would all go away if he just let the bottle win again. Just one more time. Sam had been sitting, staring, for about an hour. His mind was wracked with the images of Camilla his daughter, the one person in the world who loved him and was trying to help him - the only one who looked to him for protection and counted on him - crumpled on the floor in her bloody robe ... violated by an intruder while he slept off another drunken binge.

Then, in a fit of drunken anger, he had thrown her out - cast her out - the only person who meant anything to him. "I'm so sorry, Camilla." he wept, his hand starting to reach for the bottle. "I'm so, so sorry." Sam grabbed the bottle, and, in that moment, the bottle won. Sam began to lose himself in the whisky. After some time, he grabbed his revolver, checked the magazine and made sure it was loaded. Then placed it in his lap. Patting it with conviction. He sat there, his face stone cold. His eyes were bloodshot: despair had taken over; it was obvious what needed to happen. No one would miss him. Sam sat still in his recliner with the revolver on his thigh. Knowing his life has been such a shame to Camilla. She had Kevin to protect her now and their son Andre to worry about. She had love. She had so much life to life, and she shouldn't be burdened by his.

Doctor James Fuquan was a very private man. He took special care to assure his secrets would die with him. He did not have many friends. He trusted no one. No one that is except for his colleague Clay Stephenson. James and Clay had become close during their time in grad school. The long nights they spent studying, gave them plenty of time to build a strong friendship. Clay had been married and was always nudging his very eligible bachelor friend to date. To Clay it seemed a waste to have the looks of James and not utilize them.

James had no interest in allowing anyone to deter his focus. Long ago he devoted his life to helping others. Unfortunately, that came at his own expense. Being single was the price he paid. But that also protected his secret. Several years after he arrived in Dallas. He met a beautiful woman named Sarah Myers. Sarah was everything a man could want. Sarah was smart, she was studying to be an attorney. She was athletic, funny and had the most beautiful green eyes James had ever seen. She was studying in the library one day and James, while walking, knocked over a chair because he was staring at her. He had never before felt someone with so much radiating energy. They clicked instantly, became inseparable.

Sarah and James spent every moment together. James did his best to keep his distance. But his resistance was futile. Sarah had this magical peace about her that he craved. The sexual tension that was there was too much to bear. One evening after a long night of studying, James asked Sarah if she would like to stay the night. She agreed and what happened that night is something James will never forget. That was the first of many wonderful and sensual nights. James felt like he had finally found love. He was opening up and allowing someone into his heart. A heart that had been closed off for so long. Life was good for James, and he finally felt that he had it all. James and Sarah spent many nights together.

Their union was not perfect though. She quickly discovered that James would violently fight in his sleep. One of those nights put her in the hospital. James broke her jaw in his sleep. Sarah forgave James because she knew it was an accident. But now she had questions. James was very private about his past. He made sure to never divulge too many specific details. Focused on being a prominent attorney, Sarah was always set in truth. Throughout their relationship, Sarah just couldn't shake the feeling that James was hiding something, a secret she had to figure out. She always suspected that he most likely was a womanizer. There was no way someone as attractive and successful as him would not have many women at his disposal. And, what caused the fighting that he did when he slept? Sarah began watching James closely trying to learn what he was hiding. This made James pull away. He would rather be alone forever than to be judged by his past. They began to argue all the time. The more she wanted to know, the less he would share, it came to a point where there was more bad than good happening between them. Heartbroken, finally Sarah could take it no longer. She could not be committed to someone who could not be transparent to her. She decided it was time to leave Dallas. She had been offered a job at a law firm in Houston. That provided her the perfect opportunity to leave Dallas.

She loved James. But love could not fix the darkness and secrets looming from his past. Sarah knew she needed a clean break. She spent one last night with him then she kissed him goodbye. Without warning, Sarah disappeared. She packed up her apartment and moved to Houston. James had no idea. He called and messaged her several times the next day. With no reply, he started to worry. He decided to surprise her at her office with flowers, as he did so often. When he arrived, he was given the news that ultimately broke his heart. Sarah was gone. He knew no woman would ever accept his past. It was then when he vowed to never allow anyone into his heart ever again. Once again, God had shown James he was not a chosen one. James decided his only love would be his work and he would close himself off to love for good. He never dated again.

Chapter Twenty

Running from reality

S AM HAD SUSPECTED THURMAN, the quiet man in his anger management class, was the rapist who had violated Camilla. He was sure he was the man. The limp was his first clue. But his suspicions were confirmed beyond doubt when he saw the man leave last night. When he pulled on his jacket, the sleeve of his T-shirt gaped just enough to expose the tattoo - exactly as Camilla had described it. Thurman was the man. Sam knew it ... and no doubt remained. Sam thought he could drink away the guilt, like he had so many times before - that he could bury his shame in a pint of whisky. But no one - not even Sam - could stay drunk forever. And when he was sober - the mental anguish was more than he could stand. It left him with only one solution.

Three hours later, fifteen minutes after the start of the anger management class - Sam Thomas opened the door to the classroom and walked in. He offered no explanation for his tardiness. "Were you at your AA meeting, Mr. Thomas?" Kathryn asked. When Sam didn't respond, Kathryn told him to take a seat. "We'll discuss your punctuality after class - in private." Sam ignored her, passing the desk he usually occupied, and crossed the room walking to the last aisle where Thurman sat alone, his head scrunched down nearly level with the desktop. "Mr. Thomas!" Kathryn barked, obviously irritated, "You are holding up my class. Will you please take your seat now! "

Sam didn't even look· at her. He stopped in front of Thurman's desk, took a deep breath, then pulled a revolver from under his jacket. Before the gasps had escaped the lips of his astonished classmates, Sam brought the pistol level with Thurman's head, aiming directly between his eyes. As if knowing the outcome would not change no matter what he did, Thurman's shoulders slumped, and he exhaled his final breath. Sam pulled the trigger - the loud reverberating echo shattering the stillness that had fallen over the room. Instantly Thurman's skull exploded - the large caliber bullet blowing out the back of his head, sending bone tissue and blood splattering in a massive spray behind him. Thurman's lifeless head

- what remained of it - crashed forward, hitting the desk with a sickening thud. Kathryn screamed. The class members - the ones who were not frozen by shock - scrambled under their desks.

Smoke and an acrid odor instantly filled the room. Kathryn continued to scream hysterically. Sam finally turned to look at her, his face a blank sheet, the gun held chest high. Kathryn, anticipating the gun would now be turned on her, began flailing her arms, her high-pitched wails increasing in intensity. Sam turned his back on the teacher, facing the class, then, raising the gun slowly, he placed the barrel into his own mouth, and pulled the trigger again. Kathryn's screams were beyond hysterical. She was out of control as the pinkish, gray globs of matter, fragments and chunks of bone, and an enormous amount of blood covered the frantic woman. Kathryn's breathing accelerated as her arms swung wildly, making desperate, futile swipes at her clothing, her face, her hair, in vain attempts to rid herself of the aftermath of the brutal attack.

Sam's body twitched spasmodically for several moments, before finally stopping. The harsh, wide hole in the back of his head looked like a crater. Strands of bloody hair dangled over the cavern. Tentatively, cautiously the other students raised their heads, gawking in disbelief at the carnage - the lifeless bodies - and the woman who was thrashing around in front of them, covered in blood. It was after midnight before the hospital permitted the traumatized class members to be released. Kathryn - heavily sedated – was the last one to leave. Her husband walked beside the wheelchair as the nurse rolled her through the wide, automatic doors.

Dr. Stephenson stood beside the car, waiting to take the Thackers home. Kathryn didn't even notice him - her eyes as hard and glazed as marbles. Her husband, however, glared at Clay Stephenson, then, through clenched teeth locked tight together, he growled, "Kathryn will not be continuing with the class, doctor!" He spat out the title 'Doctor' as if it were a pejorative. Dr. Stephenson nodded. "I understand," he spoke in a soft, reverent tone. "And." Mr. Thacker's voice rose, "you haven't heard the end of this. I've already called an attorney." Of course, Clay thought. It's the new American Dream find someone you can sue preferably someone with deep pockets.

The car doors slammed shut and the Thackers sped away from the hospital. Clay Stephenson stood - watching the taillights fade away - then glanced at his watch. It was 3:47 a.m. The psychologist pulled his cell phone from his pock-et. "He said to call him anytime," Clay mumbled while he listened to the phone ring. He waited only a few minutes before James Fuquan answered his call. "Clay it's a little early for you, isn't it?" "James, I have a situation and I need your help." Responded doctor Stephenson. "What can I do for you?" groggily James asked. "I need YOU to take over Judge O'Brien's anger management class." "What's wrong with the one you have in place?"

"Oh... She's skitzing out on me. There was a shooting in the classroom, and she is a nervous wreck." "Hell, I would be too! This is more than I want to get involved with at the moment Clay." Clay responded in an elevated voice "Come on James, I NEED YOU!" James returned the bark. "Clay have you ever dealt with anyone that's been sexually abused?" Clay barked back "No, but this is perfect opportunity for you to do so!" James knew that his colleague was right. As he took a deep breath... "I will stop by your office this morning to go over the files. But what is the story on the shooting?" relieved, Clay replies "I'll explain it all when you get here."

An hour earlier, at a small diner a block from the hospital - the remaining members of Kathryn Thacker's anger management class met together for coffee ... and a discussion. "I ain't takin' all those stupid classes again," Wayne argued. "I want credit for the class. I was there. If they cancel it, I want full credit." Everyone agreed, voicing opinions in a chaotic cadence Maybeth tried to take control. "We're all shook up," she reasoned with them. "What happened tonight was horrible ... and to think we had to see it all happen. We need to think." "To hell with thinking," Kevin interrupted. "Everything in that class was bullshit. It didn't do a thing to fix any anger issues I had." "Mine either," Carla said, listening to the conversation, her phone - for once - stowed in her purse.

"I still don't like you, Wayne ... or any of you, for that matter. but we need to all stick together on this, we need to get our credit." "You are a sassy biatch," Wayne leaned across the table. "Maybe someone ought to slap that out of you." "Why are you so angry?" Carla snapped. "Come on," Maybeth urged. "We need to talk about this. If we don't stick together, we could, all pay the price." "And who made you queen?" Kevin shot her a fiery glare. "You think you're the leader because your old man was a councilman--a rapist and a child molester. Don't forget that. Helluva resumé, lady."

Maybeth fought back the tears that stung her eyes. She was not going to give in - not again! Leon had made her feel cheap and inadequate so many times. She would not go through that one more time ever! "Maybe you want to lead the discussion Kevin?" she met his stare with her own. "And if we don't do what you say, you can just beat on us 'til we all agree with you." Kevin clenched his fists and straightened his back. Almost immediately Maybeth apologized. "Kevin," her soft tone made her appear gentle and kind, "I'm sorry. That was out of line. Look - all of you - we're all after the same thing. We want credit for attending the class. None of us want to do those sessions over again, but I think we all know Mrs. Kathryn is not coming back."

"Ah, gee," Wayne dead panned. "And just when I was starting to click with her." He wiggled one eyebrow in a sexually suggestive manner and smiled broadly. His sarcasm diffused the tense atmosphere, eliciting smiles from the rest of the group, and lightening the mood. The waitress saw the smiles and darted for the table, thinking it was safe to approach them "Just keep the coffee coming," Jennifer told her when everyone declined to order. Maybeth secretly pulled a hundred-dollar bill from her purse and pressed it into the young girl's hand. "We need some time," she said "and lots more coffee." "Yes ma'am," the rail thin, blonde drawled. Then left them as speedily as she had arrived.

"OK," Wayne resumed the discussion. "How are we going to convince old man O'Brien that we deserve credit for the class, even though there's still 12 weeks to go?" Jennifer answered first. "We'll tell him - this episode we witnessed cured us of our anger issues." She said "I know I sure learned something tonight." "Yeah," Brian tried to keep the tension to a minimum, "like don't slide down in your desk." "Sam didn't shoot him because he was slouching," Kevin said, "He shot him because that bastard raped his daughter!" All eyes are riveted to Kevin. "How do you know that?" Carla asked, "he never said anything about that in class." Kevin looked off, staring out the window. "Because I just know." The exchange screeched to halt for several moments.

No one said a word when Brian spoke, his speech was serious. "Let's make sure we don't tell Judge O'Brien that part. We have to come across as being healed. And that sounds like we still have a bit of an anger issue... unresolved anger. If the judge thinks we're still angry about anything he'll throw us in jail for sure." "Maybe they'll give us another teacher." Maybeth was reasoning out loud. "Someone to take Kathryn's place." Jennifer's phone rang. It was Sable - her college roommate, Jennifer stepped away from the table to take the call.

Jennifer: "Hello Sable. "

Sable: "Hey! Jenn you wouldn't believe what just happened!"

Jennifer: "What happened?"

Sable: "Kyle and his boys just got arrested for rape and possession of drugs!"

(She was standing outside the party, watching Kyle get in the back of a police car)

Sable: "People are everywhere! Two girls were taken off in an ambulance!"

Jennifer: "It's about time they got caught. Let's see if they can pay their way out of it this time!"

Sable: "Girl this party is crazy. Well, it was a party. It's a police station now."

Jennifer: "I'll call you back."

Sable: "Are you coming through?"

Jennifer: "Nah, I'm done with that life. I'll call you later."

Jennifer walked back to the table. "If they do ..." Carla whipped her head around. "I better get credit for the classes I've already attended." "It's always about you, isn't it?" Brian snarled at her "I've already told you; I don't like you." Carla dished it right back. "I ain't like him." pointing at Wayne. "I call it like I see it - and I don't like what I see when I look at you ... or any of you." Maybeth felt like a playground monitor trying to keep the onery students from hitting each other. "Why don't we wait?" she suggested, "let's just all go to class on Monday and see what happens. Maybe the judge himself will be there - if he is, we don't wanna be late." "Judge ain't coming to the class whitey." Carla sneered. "He heard there was a shooting. No way he's coming around that class after what happened."

The group chatted for another half hour, finally concluding that Maybeth's suggestion was the best course of action. They would come to class on Monday and see what happened from there. "And let's not get into any angry fights before then - with anyone," she warned. "We all are responsible for what happens and if one messes up, then it could affect the rest of us, too." Carla blurted out again, "You tryin' to tell me how to live my life, grandma?" She was huffing and puffing and appeared to be on the verge of striking out physically. "Because I'm not the one that attacked some kid in a Lowe's store, remember? Not me. I can take care of myself." Maybeth just slumped her shoulders, exhausted. "It's been a long day," she sighed. "I'm going home. See y'all on Monday." "If I make it to Monday." Carla whispered under her breath.

Chapter Twenty-One

Gotcha

FRIDAYS ARE VISITATION DAYS at the county jail. Three weeks had passed since the DNA tests confirmed that Leon Simmons - Amber's own father - was also the father of the unborn child Amber was carrying when she took her own life. Maybeth had not visited the jail once since Leon was arrested. As if he were some hardened criminal - some terrorist posing a threat to the neighborhood - the police had shown up at the Simmons' home that morning with backup ... armed backup! Some had their guns drawn and the house was surrounded. When Maybeth tried to open the door and find out what was happening, she was nearly toppled aside as the police corralled Leon. Maybeth's lethargy since Amber's death and the volatile scene with Mark at Lowe's had prompted the doctor to keep her sedated - medicated heavily.

As the uniformed officers rushed past her with Leon in tow, she barely comprehended what was taking place. It was only after Leon had been dragged from the house in handcuffs that she realized the severity of Amber's situation ... the root of her rebellion the motivation behind her suicide. "Call the lawyer!" Leon shouted to her as they forced him into the back of the squad car. "I didn't do anything wrong." Leon was near tears as the back door slammed shut. Maybeth watched his pleading face disappear from view as the car rolled away.

"My God!" She gasped her trembling hands crushed tightly to her face. "He - he raped my little girl." The revulsion and disgust made her nauseous. Staggering backwards, she managed to find the sofa where she collapsed - a new set of tears pouring from her eyes that had already shed gallons in recent days. These tears, however, were different. These were tears of anger and outrage. It took an hour, maybe more, for Maybeth to clear her head - to begin to think clearly again. Her life - the life she had known for 18 years - was over. She heard Tammy Wynette's voice in her mind, singing "Stand By Your Man." But Maybeth knew that was not an option. She had no intention of standing by Leon. She wasn't sure she could even bear seeing him again. But she was absolutely positive she would no longer be his wife.

Ashley was gone now, too - in foster care because of the Lowe's incident. Alone, Maybeth knew her decisions right now would affect and determine the rest of her life and she was NOT going to be identified as the weak, spoiled, unaware trophy wife of a child molester. "First thing," she held up a finger like she was checking off items on a TO DO list, "I am NOT taking another one of those pills the Doctor gave me." No one else was in the house but Maybeth was speaking loudly - convincing herself - confirming her decisions with the conviction of a zealot.

She held up a second finger. "And I'm going to beg Judge O'Brien to let me take that class. I can't get Ashley back if I'm in jail and I can't get her back unless I can prove I've overcome this anger issue. Feeling better, she raised finger number three. "And I WILL get Ashley back. She's my baby - she's my world now." Two hours ago, Maybeth would have broken down thinking and talking about Ashley or Amber - but not now! Now she had a plan, and she was motivated. The fourth and final finger popped up like a soldier snapping to attention. "I WILL control my life. Every day! No one will dictate my happiness any longer. I will make it my own - and when I love again ... and I will love again it, will be on my terms and with a man who loves me and wants me.

Maybeth smiled - the first one in weeks. Leon was gone, but at least now she knew the truth. Ashley was gone, but she would get her back. She had to! Amber was gone, but now she knew why, and she could understand it. The guilt would never go away - she would carry it forever. She should have seen the signs. She should have listened to her more she should have done so much more. "That's the past." Maybeth's eyes narrowed as she focused on her future. Leon had blinded her with his insistence that he loved her and would always take care of the family. She could forgive herself for her naiveté - she had to in order to move forward - but she would never let it happen to her again. Now, if she could only forgive herself for the biggest mistake of her life.

Chapter Twenty-Two

Prison justice

LEON WAS SITTING ON the side of his bunk in his cell when he decided to call Maybeth. There was only one guy in line to use the phone, but five or six guys in the corner shooting dice. The TV was loud, it was Leon's turn to use the phone. He first called the house phone, no answer so he tried Maybeth's cell phone, still no answer. He got her voicemail instead. Leon slammed the phone down and walked back to his cell. A lil black guy they call Bam Bam was talking to one of his homies named Big T. Bam Bam said to Leon, "What are you doing fucking chomo?" "We all wanna use the phone before you break it!"

Big T said, "He breaks that phone I'm gonna break his face." Leon sat down on his bunk for a moment before walking over to the TV to catch Fox news. There was no one watching TV, when Leon decided to change the channel. One of the guys shooting dice yelled, "Who told you to touch that

TV?" Leon looked confused but didn't say anything. "Hey child molester, you hear me talking to you!?" Leon looked around with his arms folded and turned back to watch TV as if they weren't talking to him. Bam Bam walked over and got in Leon's face. "Chomos don't have rights to touch the TV. Don't touch it again!" as Big T turned it back to the channel and they both walked away. Bam Bam said, "you lucky I ain't beat yo ass already, Raping them lil kids. I hate child molesters." Leon stood there for a moment and decided to turn the TV back to Fox news. Bam Bam and Big T walked back over and beat Leon unconscious before the COs ran in and broke everyone up.

Upon his arrival in the jail - after the humiliation of a body cavity search and the demeaning attitude of the guards, Leon had been placed in general population. His pending criminal case was a high-profile case... every news channel carried the story - along with disgusting insinuations and the obligatory photograph. His cell mates recognized him the· moment he walked through the heavy iron door into the pods. Before that first, terrifying night had passed, Leon had been beaten four times. "punished" is how those inflicting the blows de-scribed it. And the guards let it happen. "We don't associate with your kind," a burly, smelly bearded man had growled, while smashing his fist into Leon's eye. "Sick bastard," he heard - over and over again. I hate child molesters. "We ought to kill you," another threatened. "You hurt helpless lil kids." Leon was beginning to hope that they did kill him.

Finally, the guards stepped in, and said "Everybody get in your cells now!" "Now!" One guard yelled and inmates ran to their cells leaving Leon on the floor in a puddle of his blood. Leon was taken to medical on a stretcher. The inmates remained in their cells. One inmate yelled "Next time we are going to kill him!" The guards walked away talking to each other, "He should have never been placed in general population."

Chapter Twenty-Three

Gaining strength

"MRS. SIMMONS, IF YOU'LL follow me, please." the guard at the jail spoke kindly, ushering Maybeth through the metal detector. After she replaced the belt around her waist and put her shoes back on, the elderly gentleman guided her down a 50-foot hallway to a large room - long and narrow - lined with small booths. Each booth had a chair, a small table and mounted on the wall, a telephone, and a sheet of thick glass separating it from an identical booth on the other side. The events in the classroom the day before -seeing the anger Sam had towards the man who had raped his daughter - ignited a rage in Maybeth. One she knew would not be quenched until she confronted the villain in her life - until she met face to face with Leon. It was a conversation she dreaded ... but, one she had to endure ... absolutely needed to endure.

Moments later, Leon was led to the chair on the opposite side of the thick glass. He was wearing an orange jumpsuit, very similar to the one she had worn so recently. He looked well - much better than she had, and she had been in jail only a few days. Leon's hair was combed neatly; he was freshly shaven; his jumpsuit appeared to have been pressed - the seams sharp and crisp. Maybeth thought she could see the lingering effects of a bruise on his cheek bone, and possibly another under his eye. Leon snatched the phone from the cradle like he had been waiting for hours at the booth. He glared at Maybeth in silence, the receiver pressed to his ear. Gradually, Maybeth lifted the handset on her side of the glass.

"Where the hell have you been?" Leon demanded. "I've been calling you ten times a day for weeks." Maybeth shook as she tried to find her voice. "It's true, isn't it?" She finally eked out the words - the words that had haunted her since the day of Amber's funeral. "What?" Leons was taken aback, not expecting her to confront him and accuse him. The glare on Maybeth's face was an accusing scowl. Gone was the blank look that would rather push problems and trials under the rug than confront them. Gone, too, was the empty person who had wandered around in a medicated stupor from the pills the doctor, at Leon's insistence, had given her. "No!" Leon asserted himself again, trying to push himself back into the role he had occupied during their marriage.

"I love you babe," he stammered. "You know that, and the kids, too. Everything I did was for them..." "Enough!" Maybeth barked so loudly other visitors craned their necks around the cubicle walls to see her. "You raped our daughter. She killed herself because she was pregnant with her father's child. My God!" Maybeth felt her body heave, her chest tightened, a panicky realization began smothering her. Verbalizing the sordid truth for the first time had shaken her, draining her of all strength and willpower. "I ... I slept with you." she shuddered, looking into the face of a man she thought she had known and loved.

"Sweetheart," Leon begged, groveling "We're a family. I ... I love you. Don't look at me like that." Maybeth slammed down the phone, unable to stomach even one more word from him. For the first time in years her vision was crystal clear. She could see who she was - and she could see who Leon was. "It's over!" she shouted at the glass, not caring if Leon - or anyone else - heard her. "It's over for good!" she hollered, her mouth making the words easy to read even if he couldn't hear them. "Mrs. Simmons," the officer was beside her in a flash. You need to pick up the phone. Talk through the phone or I'll have to ask you to leave the visitation area." Maybeth snarled at the man, then grabbed her purse. "I'm done here." she said in a huff. Before turning to leave, she gave Leon the finger.

Chapter Twenty-Four

Unequal housing

A FEW DAYS LATER Leon was released from the medical area, His hands were cuffed behind his back. He was being escorted by officer Man. Officer Man held Leon by his left bicep as they walked through the general population hallway. The hallways were lined by hordes of inmates on either side of the glass walls, many with their shirts off. All races, all ages, and all nations pounded on the walls and screamed in support for the death of the disgusting child molester. All agreeing on one thing, child molesters were the scum of the prison. They were jumping up and down and beating on the windows yelling "DIE CHOMO!" "KILL THAT FUCKING CHILD MOLESTER!" "YOU PIECE OF SHIT!! YOU WILL DIE!" As they continued to walk, Leon kept his head down. They finally made it to range B. The SHU where there were single cells. Leon asked, "Where am I going?" Officer Man responded, "Protected custody."

Lean was confused "Why?" "You can't be in general population for your own safety." Before Leon could ask "Why?" Officer Man continued, "child molesters are at high risk for death among general population. Leon responded. "How long will I be here? Can I at least use the phone?" Officer Man wasn't eager to chat. "Thirty days or so. Then you will be processed to the sex offenders' pod, and you can use the phone there. Now Mr. Simmons I need you to face the wall for me." As he unlocked the single door, he grabbed Leon by the arm again and told him to walk backwards into the cell. Officer Man then closed and locked the cell door.

A 16x16 slot opened in the middle of the door. Instructing Leon to back up and put his hands through the slot so he could get his cuffs off. While removing the cuffs, Officer Man said, "Mr. Simmons, you're a law man, a smart man. Why are the laws so lenient on white criminals? Ninety percent of child molesters are white. And the act of child molestation affects the victims for the rest of their lives. For example, you molested your daughter from the age of 7 to the age of 16. It's easy to say, if she were alive, she would have lived to be at least 65. That means she would have lived with being molested 57 of her 65 years of life! Yet child molesters are protected by so many state and federal laws. More than any other criminal. Why is that?"

Before he could answer, Officer Man continued. "The saddest part is a lot of these predators are employed to some of the highest-ranking positions at the state and federal levels. Like you, they live in the best neighborhoods in our society. You were a city councilman for 10 years and you raped your own daughter for nine of those years!" Leon responded, "I didn't hurt my daughter, I loved my daughter." Officer Man scoffed and walked away shaking his head, Leon yelled through the cell door. "I KISSED HER WITH LOVE AND AFFECTION, I TOUCHED HER WITH PASSION - SOFT AND GENTLE, I WASN'T ROUGH OR HATEFUL WITH HER! I KISSED HER IN AREAS THAT MADE HER FEEL GOOD. I DID NOT HURT HER! YOU PEOPLE JUST DON'T UNDERSTAND!!" Thirty days had passed, and Leon was being relocated to the sex offender pod. Leon was out of the gloom and no longer did he have to smell the foul stench of general population.

Chapter Twenty-Five

Privilege for the wicked

NOW RESIDING ON THE opposite side of the jail, in the CHOMO pod. The rooms were neat and tidy. The men's clothing was pressed and clean, hygiene was stressed. It was almost like home. In fact, in some ways, it was better than living with Maybeth where he had to sneak around and hide his true affections. These men understood him, and he understood them. They all had one main thing in common, they were all sex offenders, "All I ever wanted was to love my family," Leon tried to explain. Seven men, each one listening intently, nodded their agreement. "How could anyone mistake my actions for anything but love?" "We've been through it." Albert assured him. "All of us have." With each unanswered phone call to Maybeth, Leon had come to rely more and more on his 'new family'. He had found a group of men who knew the true expression of love and accepted him as an equal – as one who knew that affection could never be harmful.

Leon Simmons wobbled as he walked back to his cell unit. Where could he turn now? What would he do? "How's it going?" Albert, a fellow inmate - an elderly man with a neatly trimmed beard - asked. "Not good," Leon moaned, his head slumped forward. "She's very upset. She blames me!" Albert looped his arm around Leon's shoulder. "Society teaches them that hatred - after all we do for them." Leon nodded. Someone understood him. Actually, several of the men in the jail understood him. Meeting Albert and the others who were accused of being criminals, when all they ever did was show their affection to those they loved, was the saving grace that had enabled Leon to survive this nightmare.

"To hell with her," Leon boldly declared as he and Albert made their way back to the cell area. "Who needs her? I sure don't." "Did you ever really love her?" Albert asked him. Leon paused only a second. "No, I don't think I really did. I shared myself with her because she needed it - and I was man enough to help her meet her needs. But eventually I saw the hypocrisy in that. I went to the one I truly loved and gave her all the love I had in me. Albert squeezed Leon's shoulder. I was the best father anyone could ever have. "Of course, you were," His voice was comforting uplifting empowering.

"And then Maybeth drove her away," Leon spoke, a sudden epiphany in his voice. "Because I kept sleeping with Maybeth, Amber didn't believe me, didn't trust our love. It's Maybeth's fault. She's the one who drove Amber to do that. It was all Maybeth's fault. Not mine! It was Maybeth's fault!" Albert stopped him and squared him up to look into his eyes. "Yes," the old man said in a whisper. "Now you see. Now you know the truth." Leon's focus locked onto Albert. "And now ... " He opened his eyes wide and tightened his lips, "Now she must pay for what she did. She must pay - she must!"

Chapter Twenty-Six

A new direction

SOMBER WAS THE BEST description of the classroom as the students filed in Monday evening. The blood and mess had been cleaned up and the floors scoured, but the memories were far from erasable. Each person, entering on trembling legs, avoided eye contact with each other - but paused a moment, as if held in their step - and peered at the spot where the fatal altercation had taken place. Almost reverently they each stepped around the location where the two bodies had fallen. It was ten minutes past 6 when Brian spoke, breaking the respectful silence. "Nobody's coming," he softly concluded. "We're forgotten. We're toast. Judge ain't gonna see no certificate and we're all going to jail." Everyone turned to look at Brian.

Maybeth started to speak, but was interrupted when a sturdy, tall, distinguished looking black man entered the room and walked to the front. He carried an air of confidence, assurance and authority - a commanding aura that caught the attention of each person. "Hello class, my name is Dr. James Fuquan. The man introduced himself in a voice that seemed to suck the breath from each one in the room. "I am purposefully late by a few minutes, assuming you would appreciate a few moments of silence before we tackle the essence of our attendance here." Dr. Fuquan spoke with an eloquence that attested to both his education and his self-esteem.

In complete contrast to Kathryn Thacker, James Fuquan was in charge and left no doubt about it. "As I'm sure you have surmised," Fuquan continued after a short pause, "I will be your facilitator for the remainder of your class. We have a lot to cover - a lot to accomplish - so I suggest we waste little time on the past and move forward in our effort to resolve the issues that have mandated your attendance here. I will, however, entertain a few questions, since the circumstances which brought me into your midst are unique and possibly even traumatizing. Does anyone have a question or a concern?"

Like a prize fighter feeling out his opponent, the class members cautiously eyed this new guy, each wondering what he could possibly say that would help them. It seemed unlikely that this Dr. Fuquan had ever had an anger issue - or any kind of problem at all; his demeanor exuded confidence and privilege he carried himself with an alluring charisma and he seemed the visual definition of success. It was doubtful he had ever had a bad day or ever faced a serious challenge in his apparently charmed life.

Wayne Wade spoke first. "Yeah, I got a question," he curled the corner of his mouth, showing disrespect for the 'rich guy' who was attempting to ride in on a white horse and save the floundering underlings from themselves. "What happened to Ms. Kathryn. Why is she not coming back?" Fuquan's stoic countenance didn't change. "Ms. Thacker has opted not to continue with the class. Dr. Stephenson, Ms. Thacker's supervisor, did not want to cancel the class and force you to face Judge O'Brien without completing what he ordered, so I have been asked to mediate the remainder of the course, allowing each of you to earn the certificate the Judge will ask to see." "What's your qualifications to do that?" Brian's tone matched the condescension o. Wayne "I suppose, I was chosen because no one else would do it." Dr. Fuquan made no attempt to hide the truth. "I do, though, carry the title of Doctor of Psychology, so I believe that gave Dr. Stephenson the confidence to trust me with the class. I will be honest with you - I have never before led a class on Anger Management, but I have counseled a number of individuals who suffered from that problem.

"You look pretty old," Jennifer was sizing him up, his broad shoulders and handsome physique which was complimented by his handsome features - all of which appealed to her and gave her small sensations of lust. "Are you sure you can handle us?" she asked, a bit mischievously. Jennifer's question brought snickers from her classmates, each one glancing between Jennifer and the new, tall teacher before them. Dr. Fuquan waited for the chuckles and under-the-breath comments to die down, then said, "I make no claims to 'handle' you, Ms. Potter, but I will promise you I will do all I can to help you find a way to handle yourself." His comments, naturally, brought another round of snide, suggestive remarks.

Jennifer bristled. "Hey!" she demanded, like an attorney cross-examining a hostile witness. "What are you saying? I don't handle myself. I don't need to do that." "Ain't nothin' wrong with that," Brian soothed her. "I don't do that!" Jennifer raised her voice. "Maybe you do, but I do not!" Dr. Fuquan let the banter continue only a moment, then he spoke up. "Jennifer, you assumed I had some ulterior meaning in my words." "Sure sounded like you did," she said, still seething. "And that made you angry?" he asked. "Sure, it did," Jennifer clenched the desktop. "Everyone in this room thought you were hinting at something." Dr. Fuquan moved slightly closer to the students but kept his focus on Jennifer. "And why do you care what they think?" he asked.

"Yeah," Carla half laughed. "Just don't like nobody and you don't care what they think." "I ain't like you," Jennifer snarled across the room at Carla, who was listening while examining her fingernails. "Too bad," Carla said "Life's a lot easier when you hate everybody." "And Ms. Warfield does hate everybody," Dr. Fuquan took her side. "She hates them so much she doesn't care what they think when she wears her Prada shoes and designer jeans to an anger management class oh, and the $800 handbag. She doesn't care so much that she won't leave the house without dressing up, and she sure doesn't care what you think of her while she sits in the beauty salon getting her hair done and her nails manicured." Amid some chuckles Carla creased her brow. "Hey, there's nothing wrong with looking nice - no harm in that. I don't have to like anyone to want to look nice." She sounded defensive and nervous.

"No," Dr. Fuquan agreed. "Yet . . ." he paused, turning his attention to Carla. "Who are you looking nice for?" Carla frowned deeper, then said, "For ME!" "Uh-huh," Dr. Fuquan nodded unconvincingly. "Of course, you never actually see yourself - except in the mirror – whereas all the people you profess to hate, have to look at you all day long. Seems like you're going through a lot of trouble to make the hated ones feel more comfortable." Now the entire class was on the edge of their seats, watching and listening. "So, tell me, Ms. Warfield," Dr. Fuquan continued when Carla didn't respond, "who are you really trying to impress here?" He looked around the room slowly. "Is it Brian or Wayne?" Carla was scowling like she had met her direst enemy. "Or perhaps is it Mrs. Simmons?" Carla nearly jumped out of her desk. "I am not a lesbian," she slammed her fist on the desktop. "And I don't do white guys!" She shot another hateful glance at Wayne, who was listening and didn't try to out talk her.

Dr. Fuquan stared directly at her. "Don't do white guys anymore, you mean," he seemed to correct her. "Not after what happened with your adopted family, correct?" Carla's face was shaking, and a tear leaked from her eye. Dr. Fuquan softly laid a hand on Carla's shoulder, then removed it and returned to the front of the room. "Everybody in here has a story - a horrible, unfair story. We will not hide behind those stories but confront them. Because of what happened to each of you some more horrible than any torturous death - you feel your lives have been stolen - your innocence shattered your future blemished." He had every eye watching him. Sitting down on the edge of the teacher's desk, then Dr. Fuquan made eye contact with each person. They seemed torn, anxious to hear what he had to say next - apprehensive that he might single them out and expose their hidden secrets.

"You are partially correct," Dr. Fuquan nodded, speaking in a tone that exuded confidence and knowledge "You have had moments stolen from you. And it has been tragic." With everyone seeming to hold their breath, Dr. Fuquan placed both palms on the desktop, using his arms to brace himself as he leaned forward, giving more intimacy to the conversation. "But," he lowered his voice, "if someone steals something from a store, the merchant doesn't just open the doors and tell that person to steal everything else he has." A couple of slight nods indicated his message was getting through. "Those stolen moments are gone - you cannot bring them back."

He rose, standing tall before them, then slowly moved down the aisle as heads turned to follow him. "But you control the moments that lie ahead. Are you willing to open your future and let the world steal those moments, too?" He asked, "Are you going to hide behind your past and let your future rot on the vine?" The students were all paying close attention. It was Maybeth Simmons who spoke first. "How is hating what happened to us damaging our future? I will never stop hating what my husband did." Dr. Fuquan pivoted and his gaze fell on Maybeth.

"Suppose" he said, "that a man walked into your house un-invited - just marched through the front door carrying a pail of sloppy, smelly, wet garbage. And suppose he took that garbage and dumped it - all the oozing, stinking mess - right in the middle of your living room carpet. What would you think of that what would you do?" Aghast, Maybeth's eyes widened. "I'd ... I'd be outraged! I would ... I would... " Wayne's gruff voice broke in. "I'd take a gun and put it to his head and tell him to clean it up." Dr. Fuquan shifted to look at Wayne. "Of course. Anyone might do the same and feel justified in doing so. Now," he arched his eyebrows, "suppose this same man did clean it up - in fact, he cleaned it up so well that the carpet was cleaner now than it was before he entered. Maybe he even replaced the rug. Now how do you feel?"

Brian held his breath, unwilling to expose his feelings. "I would ... " Maybeth squeaked from beside him, "I would forgive him, but" "Now wait," Dr. Fuquan cut her off. "We're only talking about the carpet, right now. We'll get to the other issues soon." He was holding up his hand like a traffic cop stopping a car. "I believe," he continued, "that even though you came out ahead on the carpet example, that for the rest of your life, you would tell the story of the crazy man who dumped garbage on your floor." The tension in the room was thick. Everyone was closely following what was being said.

"And what good would that do?" Dr. Fuquan asked, "To talk about the garbage ... forever? Yet we do it every day. We relive all the garbage in our lives each day and wonder why we feel so angry. People are always dumping garbage in our minds if nowhere else - and that garbage piles up, affecting us physically and emotionally. Tell me - how many more stolen moments are you willing to give up? How much longer are you willing to let the front door be open so the world can dump their garbage on you? How much more of your future are you comfortable with losing? Is it OK with you if this garbage dumper in your life keeps on dumping his garbage on you for the rest of your life? Because that is exactly what is happening each day you hang on to those feelings and relive the hurt someone put on you."

Dr. Fuquan paused - looking at each student intently – then looked at his watch. "That's it for tonight," he said. "Tomorrow, be on time." And as quickly as he had entered, Dr. Fuquan was gone - leaving the students in a somber silence, sitting in the classroom.

Chapter Twenty-Seven

Be careful who you judge

T HE DINER SEEMED THE most logical place to go following the class and all six students slid into the oversized booth in the farthest corner of the restaurant. "I need more than just coffee," Carla motioned for the waitress. "I need some pie ... or something sweet. That man made me so ang... " she caught herself and didn't finish the word. "Yeah," Wayne agreed with her. "He comes in wearing his $10, 000 watch and jumps on you about your shoes!" "Maybe ... maybe it's some lame technique," Brian looked like he was in pain as he tried to find his thoughts. "You know - some college trickery that's supposed to work on us .. some trick the shrinks learn for the idiots they counsel." "Or maybe ... " Maybeth was concentrating hard. "Maybe he is just interested in us and knows us." "You saying you think he's perfect?" Carla opened the wounds of the classroom again.

"No," Jennifer answered for her. "He just found it easy to pick on us because he probably has never had a bad day in his life and he probably detests anyone who isn't – well, who doesn't fit his image of perfection." "So," Carla assessed what was said, "you're saying that he thinks he is perfect." "Well, yeah?" Maybeth was still wincing. "He had a good point, though. I mean about the garbage and the future and all." Wayne leaned across the table. "Getting over what happened to us is a lot harder than getting over someone spilling some trash on your floor." Brian had been silent just listening and processing. "How 'bout we punish them for what they did first," he said, "Then we might could forget about what they did ... but not before." Maybeth shook her head. "I don't think that's what he meant. We won't forget - certainly won't forgive - if all we think about is getting even. Not even after they are punished." "Sure, will feel good at the time," Brian said and everyone joined in to agree with him.

Maybeth continued moving her head from side to side. "I don't know seems like such a waste. You remember that Goldman guy that got killed with Nicole Simpson?" The table nodded, her reference to OJ Simpson still fresh in their minds. Maybeth continued, "His father has spent every day hating OJ and doing all he can to 'get even' with him." "Yeah, so?" Brian asked, "The guy killed his son. What's a father supposed to do?" "I'm not sure," Maybeth admitted. "And I'm not sure Dr. Fuquan knows either. But I do know that I saw Mr. Goldman on TV a few weeks ago ... and he looks old - really, really, old. And very sad." "Like someone had stolen his moments ... stolen his future." Jennifer put the pieces together. "Yes," Maybeth nodded, not looking at anyone. Carla cleared her throat. "I need some pie," she said.

Chapter Twenty-Eight

Wanting to be accepted

CARLA WAS THE LAST one to leave the diner. She poked around at the half-eaten pie on her plate, sipped slowly from the coffee cup and even offered to pick up the tab for the evening's discussion, hoping everyone would leave before her. She didn't want to walk with anyone - didn't want to talk to anyone. Her insides felt as if a jump rope got tangled up in there but kept swinging around and around anyway, knotting up more and more with each rotation. When the booth was empty, Carla sat there alone - a tear welling up in her eye. She fought to keep it back; her throat so thick she could barely swallow. She didn't want to get old - like Mr. Goldman or spend her life hating - but she had to ... she had to hate them She had to!

"How can I forgive them?" she murmured. The conversation - the garbage story by Dr. Fuquan - all of it hit home sharply. Memories she wanted to bury rose again to the surface, riding on the back of the anger and hatred she had refused to relinquish. She could still hear their voices - as clear now as the day she was adopted ... as clear as the day she was rushed from the only real home she had ever known, leaving her adopted parents behind - fleeing a situation she could no longer endure for the second time. "Her name is Carla," Mr. Warfield had said, holding her in his arms the day the adoption was final. Carla was 8 years old and had never been held by a white man before. In fact, she couldn't recall ever being held ... or loved ... by anyone. "Get outta my face" was the most common phrase she had heard since birth. When her mother was arrested for drug possession and distribution, Carla landed in an orphanage, which is where the Warfields found her.

"She sure is dark," Donny, the older of the two Warfield boys said, gawking at her like she was a museum piece. "Yeah," Ricky laughed. Donny was 15 and Ricky was nearly 14 both big for their age ... and surly. "You boys treat little Carla like a Princess, you hear?" Mr. Warfield scolded. "She's our beautiful princess and she's now your sister." "Ain't my sister," Donny shook his head violently. "No way!" "You'll treat her as a lady - as your sister," their father warned, "or you'll be punished. That' s the way it is and always will be from now on. Carla is a Warfield and she's your sister." It took Carla a very short time to feel the resentment from her 'brothers'. Both boys seemed to hate her. Mr. Warfield went out of his way to cater to her needs. He bought her special presents from work - a mechanical pencil or a stuffed toy from the store or a new fanny pack to carry her school supplies. Donny and Ricky shot her evil, glaring looks each time she got another gift - stares that frightened her. But she said nothing. As long as Mr. Warfield was near, she felt safe.

Nearly a year passed in the Warfield home. The tensions between Carla and her brothers was never verbalized, but she could feel their presence - and feel their hostility. The fawning Mr. Warfield did over her even made Carla feel uncomfortable at times, and she often wished there was some way she could get him to pay more attention to his sons. The more she matured as a woman, the more sensitive she was to the treatment Donny and Ricky were receiving from Mr. Warfield. That was probably the reason she agreed to go with Donny and Ricky that first afternoon - to mend some fences, try to bridge the gap.

"We're going down to the sandlot Carla." Ricky said, his voice as kind and sweet as she had ever heard it. "Why don't you come along with us. We can talk and watch the kids play ball." Mr. Warfield - and at times, Mrs. Warfield - were the only adults who had ever treated her kindly. Though Donny and Ricky weren't yet adults, they were big. Anxious to have them as allies and friends - excited to be included in their group - Carla quickly agreed to tag along. There was no game at the sandlot that afternoon. Both the field and the 'SNACK SHACK' were vacant. The chit chat along the way had been pleasant enough to where Carla never realized the trap the boys had laid for her.

When Donny wiggled his way into the empty Snack Shack, Ricky nearly pushed Carla through the same small opening. Out of the view of anyone who might pass by, and any sounds muffled by the Snack Shack walls and the vast open space between the ballfield and the nearest house Donny and Ricky both told Carla it was time she showed them how much she loved them. Frightened and alone, Carla at first confused When the boys threatened her, she timidly did as she was told - disrobing in front of them. Giggling and laughing while Carla tried to cover herself, Donny acted first. He lunged - grabbed her - and pinned her to the floor.

"You yell one time ... " he growled as he forced her legs apart, "and I'll bust your head wide open. make sure you never walk again, either." Carla wasn't sure what was happening. She wanted to scream as Donny clutched at her - squeezed her - then forced himself inside her. The pain ... the humiliation. She remembered his words - his threat - and she wept. Wept as silently as she could but she wept. When Donny was finished, Ricky wasted no time in taking his turn. When both boys were done, Donny snarled at her. "Get your clothes on," he ordered. "And you mention this even once and we'll kill you, understand?" "Kill you dead,' Ricky added, as if she didn't know what killed meant. "And get used to this, too," Donny told her. "Long as yer our sister, you'll be giving us lots of 'family' benefits." Ricky laughed a hyena's laugh - a sound Carla could never erase from her memory. And she would never forget their brutality - the harshness of what they did - or the way they both ran off, leaving her to stumble home alone.

The rapes continued for more than a year - long enough for Carla to plan her escape - long enough for her to develop a hatred for all white boys - long enough for her to wonder if she was even capable of having a relationship with anyone ... ever! Would she see Donny's wicked smile every time she was intimate with a man? Would Ricky's laughter ring in her head when someone told her he loved her? Was she even lovable? Would anyone want her? Now? Nice clothes, designer shoes, expensive accessories - were the only tools of self-esteem Carla knew. She would show the world she was something - she would look like every man's dream ... even if she hated every man she saw.

"I just can't forgive them," she mumbled, tears dropping onto the paper placemat. "I can't give up my anger. It's what I live for ... the revenge. It's the only defense mechanism I have left." As she sat alone in the booth, Carla saw Donny's face again. The teeth were baring viciously at her, warning her, promising her "If you tell a soul about this ... I'll kill you." Carla had absolutely no doubt Donny would carry through with his threat. That's why - for years now - her motivation each day was to avoid being seen by him ... that's why she dressed up so nicely .. why she presented herself as someone he would never recognize. Because Carla knew, if they found her, she would have to kill him ... or be killed by him. From across the diner a lone man, his face obscured by the menu he held high, watched Carla as she finally rose and left the booth. Once she stepped outside - into the dark of the night - he, too, slid from his seat, and left behind her.

Chapter Twenty-Nine

Trash

THE ANGER MANAGEMENT STUDENTS were pensive as they entered the classroom the following day - but punctual. A seriousness reflected on each face as they filed into the room. The garbage on the floor example coupled with the discussion in the diner, had created a lot of anxiety and personal thinking. Each was eager to see what kind of follow-up Dr. Fuquan had, and their judgment of the man was still on hold. "He's articulate and charismatic," Maybeth had surmised when she tried to describe him to her friend. "But most of us don't trust him." Allison, her friend, wrinkled her nose. "He's just doing it for the money, right? A lot of those shrinks are that way," "No." a concentrated look crossed Maybeth's face. "I don't get that feeling from him. It's .. I'm not sure." "I'll bet he just wants to keep his distance, so he won't be blamed for what happened – you know- the shooting and all." Allison popped the gum in her mouth as she spoke.

Maybeth shook her head again. "He doesn't strike me as someone who is concerned about anything." She paused, then her eyes shot open. "Maybe that's it. Maybe he's just so rich and so spoiled ... never had to deal with our kind of issues. Yes!" She nodded convincingly. "I'm sure that's it." Dr. Fuquan didn't even mention the previous day's topic. He immediately launched into a story, using Maybeth as his example again. "What kind of pie do you like, Mrs. Simmons?" Maybeth smiled and drawled, "Give me a thick wedge of Dutch apple pie any day, and I'm a happy eater." "Huh," Jennifer snorted, "Like you've ever had more than one piece of pie in your life. You're so skinny you gotta run around in the shower just to get wet 'cept for your boobs." The class laughed and Maybeth arched her back, grinning, showing off her bustline.

"Ahem." Dr. Fuquan cleared his throat. then went on with his example. "Suppose. Mrs. Simmons, that Furr's cafeteria had the best Dutch apple pie in the world, and you have a craving for a slice of it. You've got thirty minutes for lunch - just enough time to go to Furr's and grab a sandwich and a piece of your favorite pie - and get back to work." "I like this story," Maybeth cackled. Dr. Fuquan smiled politely. "Furr's however," he said, "is packed. The line waiting to get a tray is long You think about going somewhere else, but the thoughts of that pie on your tongue quells any notion of departure." "That's me," Maybeth confessed. "I'd risk being late for work if I really wanted the pie." "So, you wait."

Dr. Fuquan glanced at Maybeth but made eye contact with the rest of the class. Everyone was paying attention "So," the psychologist paused, "you put a few items on your tray - a sandwich, a salad ... then you come to the desserts. You look, you search ... but no Dutch Apple pie." Maybeth frowns and moans the others giggle. "You even catch the attention of the dessert matron, and she explains that they had Dutch Apple pie, but apparently every piece had been purchased." Another faux moan from Maybeth and Dr. Fuquan went on with the story-

"After you pay, Mrs. Simmons you see that the entire place is full. Nary an empty seat in the dining hall. Finally, you spot a lone chair at a table - a table for two - with only one person sitting there. He is an elderly man, dining alone. You politely inquire about the empty seat, and he cordially invites you to join him." "Uh-huh," Carla pipes up, "I see where this is going. The old geezer is going to hit on her, right?" Dr. Fuquan holds up his hand. When it was quiet, he continued. "So, Mrs. Simmons, you sit down across from him and the first thing you notice, sitting on his tray, is a piece of Dutch Apple pie." "Aaaahhh," several students intoned. "You're upset, aren't you, Mrs. Simmons?" Dr. Fuquan asked rhetorically. "You sit there- eyeballing the pie, the only reason you came to Furr's in the first place. Your food has lost its savor with the heated emotions rising within you. 'He probably got the last piece' you tell yourself. 'For sure he got MY piece' right?"

He raised an eyebrow and peeked at her. "A few minutes later," the Dr. told the attentive class," This man wipes his mouth on his napkin, drops it on his tray, stands up - and walks away - leaving the Dutch Apple pie untouched." "That would be mine," Jennifer spoke up. "I'm all over that." Dr. Fuquan smiled serenely and looked at Jennifer. "Maybeth looks at it don't you?" he asks. "She looks long and hard. Figuring he left it. Deciding to just taste it, just a bite. So, you slip your fork across the table and carve off a chunk. Oh MY! It is so good! Probably the best Dutch Apple pie you have ever eaten - and you have eaten a lot of it, am I correct?" Maybeth nods firmly.

"The crust is moist," the doctor said with a lick of his lips. "The apples and the seasoning are baked to perfection. This is why you came to Furr's. You feel the deliciousness slide down your throat. You glance around the room - no one is watching. Carefully, as subtly as you can, you slide the plate containing the Dutch Apple pie off the old man's tray ... and on to yours. Now ... now the Dutch Apple pie is YOURS! Savoring every morsel, you consume the pie - scraping the plate to get every bit, barely able to open your eyes - so intense is the ecstasy of the pie. As you raise your fork to your mouth for the last bite, you open your eyes and look up. There, to your astonishment, standing next to the table, cradling a dish of ice cream in his hands - is the old man."

"Aaaah!" the class hooted. "The old man looks down at you," Dr. Fuquan said, "and he says, "I always wait to get my ice cream until after I've eaten my meal so it won't melt, and I can eat it with my pie." "Busted!" Brian heehawed. "That old man's gonna smack you." "Oh, no," Maybeth covered her mouth with her hand. Brian reined in a smile. "What's that got to do with anger management?" he asked, his deep voice cutting through the din of the class.

"Excellent question," Dr. Fuquan nodded at Brian. "Let's find out." He stood from where he was seated on the corner of the desk, directly in front of Maybeth, and paced across the floor. "That Dutch Apple pie was delicious - Mrs. Simmons loved every bite - until it was gone, and the old man returned. Then, no matter how much she enjoyed it, she would have done anything - given anything - to put it back. All she had lusted for - all her desires - were dashed in that moment of regret a moment that would reside in her subconscious forever."

"Yeah, so?" Brian still frowned. "No one got angry." Dr. Fuquan measured his words carefully. "Delicious," he repeated. "But nevertheless forbidden." He waited a moment as the class pondered his words, then said, "Each of you have a piece of Dutch Apple pie sitting on a tray in front of you metaphorically speaking You each have a passion - a lust - an overwhelming desire to gain revenge on someone - on the individual who harmed you the one you blame for your problems. You may even find nourishment from your plans to execute this revenge." Now the class was quiet waiting thinking... listening. "I'm certainly not saying revenge - the revenge you seek - is unjustified," the Dr's voice was fluid yet stern. "It is probably more deserved than anything you have ever known. And it is a delicious piece of pie - in your eyes. Yes, very delicious."

He paused again, a lengthy lull, amid the stillness around him. "But, nevertheless, forbidden." Every ear was tuned to Dr. Fuquan. "Acting out this revenge, a deliberate manifestation of violence on another person, will be the most distasteful dessert you have ever eaten. Delicious in appearance, but fatal in execution - and the fatality will be you." Everyone wanted to speak - wanted to tell him that he didn't understand the agony they had suffered - wanted to ridicule him for being so out of touch with people who have truly been harmed - wanted to mock his perfect life and explain how revenge was the antidote for the suffering they were experiencing. But no one did. Instead, Brian spoke - softly and reverently. "How do we combat those feelings?" he asked. "Maybeth may still want, the pie. How do we eliminate the desire?"

Dr. Fuquan felt a grin burst out inside him, but he kept his voice stoic. "You're a weightlifter, Brian, I can see by the definition in your muscles" Brian - who ordinarily would have struck a pose, strutting his physique - merely nodded. "Tell me," Dr. Fuquan focused on Brian, "if you could lift 100 pounds with your right arm alone," he raised his right arm as if he were curling a dumbbell, "and 100 pounds with your left arm alone," he repeated the charade, "how much could you lift with both of your arms combined?" Brian thought only a second. "Probably. I mean at least 300 pounds." "That's right," Dr. Fuquan said, scanning the others. "Two arms working together can lift much more than the total of each one separately."

The class was in agreement and watched as Dr. Fuquan pulled a sharpie from his pocket. sliding a piece of paper from the podium, he wrote on it, then held it up to the class. The sign read '1 + 1 = 3' "I guess we could say this is a true statement, from what Brian just, told us, no matter what mathematics tells us, right? At least when it comes to weightlifting." Everyone nodded. "It was 1 + 1 = 4 with me and that dirtbag of a husband I had." Maybeth grinned as the class laughed. "It's the same principle, Brian." Dr. Fuquan returned his focus to the question Brian had asked. "You can try to fight your urges for revenge alone. I can try to fight mine alone. We might even be moderately successful, individually, but together," he tapped the crude sign,

"1+1=3. We can accomplish so much more as a team. You and Maybeth ... Wayne and Carla, Brian and Jennifer. Whatever the makeup of each one - combined with another - we exponentially enhance our potential for success." The doctor watched the class for a moment, thinking he could almost see the wheels turning in their minds - the gears meshing and changing ... and grinding too. "Those are your new assigned companions." Dr. Fuquan said. "Each one will... " "What?" Kevin gasped. "You mean like partners or something?" "Or something," Dr. Fuquan nodded. "You're trying to avoid jail. This is the assignment. You'll meet with the person I paired you with - tonight or tomorrow - and listen to their story. Find ways together to help each other - combine your strengths - and navigate through the maze of confusion you feel against those who have harmed you."

"This is lame." Jennifer snapped. "Me and the white boy?" Carla nearly shouted, her face a twisted mess of sour looks. "I ain't talkin' to nobody." Wayne insisted, shrinking in his desk. Dr. Fuquan leaned forward, his piercing eyes penetrating so deeply, the room went instantly quiet. "You're not cut out for jail, Wayne "he said with authority. "None of you are." "How would you know, rich boy?" Kevin snarled, his upper lip quivering in anger. Dr. Fuquan stared at him a moment. "You'll come prepared tomorrow to discuss what you've learned about the advantages of the partner you have been assigned." Turning his back to the class he said, "I'm going to hang this sign on our wall." He pulled a piece of tape from the dispenser and attached the paper to the plaster. "And we'll see you all tomorrow."

Chapter Thirty

Learning to trust

CARLA SAT RIGID IN her desk. Dr. Fuquan had left without saying another word. Wayne was fidgeting, his body twitching each time he looked at Carla. "Come on, guys." Maybeth's cheerful lilt sang across the room. "Let's get us some coffee and talk." Kevin analyzed the jovial, attractive woman, then said, grinning, "And Some Dutch apple pie, too?" Maybeth beamed. "And I'll buy."' Jennifer slowly sauntered over to where Brian had stood next to his desk. "Guess we never got formally introduced," she shyly extended her hand. "I'm Jennifer." Brian sighed, then smiled, then shook her hand. "We can make this fast ... if you want." he suggested. Jennifer lowered her eyes and said, "I'm in no real hurry." A moment later Carla and Wayne were alone in the room. It was the first time Carla had been alone with a white boy since Donny and Ricky.

"Awkward," Carla mumbled without looking up. Desperately she wanted to talk to someone ... to have a compatible partner like the others had. Why had he given her this guy? Wayne was arrogant, smart mouthed ... and white! "Very," Wayne agreed with her. The silence extended, nether budging in their stubbornness. It was Wayne who finally relented. "Look, I don't need to tell anyone 'bout nothin - my problems are my own and I don't need to tell nobody nothin'." "Anything," Carla muttered. Wayne looked at her. "Huh?" "You don't need to tell anyone anything. You said nothing. It's a double negative. You don't use a double negative in English, but you do in Spanish." Wayne just gawked at her. "Are you like - smart or something? Did I say that right. I mean correct ... uh..." Carla smiled. "Yeah, you said it correctly. And I'm ..." "That's a gorgeous smile," Wayne interrupted her. "And I'm not just sayin that. I know you don't like me - or any white guys at all - but you should smile more. You're beautiful when you do."

Carla's lips opened again - another smile. "Guess we should start over - I have no desire to go to jail." "How 'bout we get some pie, too?" Wayne offered. "I know just the place." "Banana cream?" "Your choice, my lady," Wayne said, a gentleness in his tone. He put out his hand and Carla took it, rising from the desk.

Chapter Thirty-One

Opening the door

"KEVIN YOU'RE A HANDSOME young man." Maybeth told the sulking boy as they sat across from each other at the table. Maybeth had ordered Dutch Apple pie but was just picking at it. "You should be happy. You're young, your whole life is ahead of you. But you seem so angry, all the time. May I ask why?" Kevin squinted at her. "Why do you care? You're a rich, white lady. Is this some service project you have to do? Is there some reason you care about me?" Maybeth tried to act unfazed. Her efforts at congeniality had been so gruffly rebuffed it had stifled her courage. ""I care," she said honestly, "because your attitude reminds me of my daughter ... my beautiful Amber." "Oh, I'll bet her life is really tragic," Kevin 's voice was heavy with sarcasm. "She having trouble deciding between the BMW and the Mercedes coupe for her birthday this year?"

Maybeth steeled her eyes, forcing back a tear. "Amber is dead," she said, a slight surprise registering in Kevin's face. "She took her own life - hung herself - because her father had been molesting her for several years ... and I was so blinded by my own life - my needs and wants - that I didn't see it or refused to see it." It may have been the first time he had ever been completely speechless. He just stared at the woman - old enough to be his mother - reassessing all he had ever thought about her. Filling the silence, Maybeth said, "I don't want your sympathy, I want to find a way to prevent someone else from doing what Amber did. I don't want anyone to have to go through what I did ... and what she did. That's why I want to know about you. Maybe it will help me understand Amber - for sure it will help me be the friend you need right now.

Kevin sat another minute quietly, then said, "Why shouldn't I be angry? Life has kicked me in the balls since I was a kid. Then, when I finally find someone who loves me – loves me the way I am and for who I am - she gets raped, right in her own home. And I couldn't do a thing about it." Maybeth put her small hand on his, letting her fingers knead the top of Kevin's hand. "Is ... are you ... in the class ..." She asked, "Because of Thurman?" Kevin met her eyes. "Yeah ... er ... no ... I mean ... sorta," It had been years since he had allowed his emotions to surface, but Kevin could feel his heart pounding in his throat as Maybeth spoke. He forced a slight cough. "I did something horrible to someone, yes, but he deserved it, and I didn't get sent to the class for that. The judge ordered me to take the class - or go to jail - because I went on a spree ... I guess."

When Maybeth tacitly told him to continue, Kevin said, "I destroyed a lot of property ... after what happened to Camilla. Houses, cars, things like that. I was so angry after the rape I couldn't control myself." "Believe me," Maybeth squeezed his hand, "I know exactly what you mean. I could have torn down a building when I found out the truth about my husband." Kevin shifted gears, anxious to avoid baring too many of his feelings." What did you do? Did you hit him?" Maybeth shook her head. "He was already in jail when I learned the truth. I didn't visit him for weeks."

Kevin raised his eyebrows "How did it go when you finally went go see him?" Maybeth grinned, then leaned forward, like she was sharing a secret. "I flipped him the bird," she whispered. "First time I ever did that." Kevin smiled. "You? Ms. Perfect? I woulda paid to see that!" "Perfect?" Maybeth echoed his word, "I am far from perfect." An awkward silence was broken when Kevin asked, "Why do you suppose Fuquan put us together?" Creasing her brow, Maybeth pondered a moment. "Are you uncomfortable being seen with me Kevin?"

Kevin shrugged. "It's not that it's just that ... you know, the others are a lot more my age. Lot more in common. No offense, but you're from another generation. You probably don't even like rap music."

"Oh, God no!" Maybeth's body shook like she had a chill. "It's not really music ... is it?" Kevin avoided a musical confrontation. "Just woulda been more logical to pair me up with someone else, don't you think?" "Maybe ..." Maybeth was still deep in thought. "Maybe Dr. Fuquan wanted each pair to be a racial mix. You know - Carla and Wayne, Brian and Jennifer, maybe he wants us to see how we do in that environment." Kevin smiled. "Actually, as I talk to you, I'm kinda glad he did put us together, I mean. I never really had a mom, and those others are young - not mature, I mean ... not serious. I need to learn to be the man Camilla needs me to be. I kinda think you can help me get there."

Maybeth beamed. "You can call me Mom anytime you want." Four blocks away, Carla and Wayne concluded their meeting in the small diner with smiles and a handshake, something neither thought was possible two months ago. Wayne offered to walk her home, but Carla declined. "I live close," she lied. Her nice, expensive wardrobe did not match the tiny, rundown apartment she rented in one of the seedier parts of town. And she didn't want anyone to see it. When they parted, each going their separate ways, another figure, clothed in black, slipped out of the alley and followed Carla.

Acceptance and forgiveness

O NE BY ONE, AS each of the students entered the classroom the next day, they quickly pulled up and stared at Dr. Fuquan. Some stood in the doorway - mouth agape, reluctant to go in. Others slithered down an aisle and dropped into a seat, never once taking their eyes off the display in front of the room. Dr. Fuquan was standing at the head of the classroom. In front of him was a table, draped with a sheet, covering something that resembled a body - a human body! The Dr. himself, was wearing hospital scrubs - complete with sanitary hat, rubber gloves, and paper boots covering his shoes. Around his neck hung a stethoscope and a face mask was positioned on his head, waiting to be used. When all six students had finally come into the room and had looked back and forth from the display in front of them to each other several times,

Dr. Fuquan finally spoke. "Tonight, " he opened his speech seriously and gravely, "we will be performing surgery. Our patient is extremely ill - and unless our surgery is successful, death is the unavoidable outcome."

Six sets of eyes bulged. Carla shot him a disgusting stare. Brian looked doubtful. "You don't have a real corpse under there, do you?" Dr. Fuquan met Brian's gaze, pausing. Without humor, he said, "NO - I do not have a corpse under here. I have six of them " "What?" Jennifer almost gagged. "I don 't like blood. You need to know that." "He said, six," Wayne shot her a look. "Don't you get it? Six! There are six of us ... he is saying we are all under the sheet. We are the corpses."

Under the stares of each student, Dr. Fuquan confirmed Wayne's conclusion. "Very astute, Mr. Wade," he said. "The demonstration is intended to parallel the critical condition of each of your lives." "Critical condition?" Kevin challenged him. "You saying we're all about to die of something ... I mean ... soon?" "I'm not saying it," the Dr. steadied his voice. "I am guaranteeing it! Oh, your body may continue breathing, but any resemblance to living will be a legend." When everyone started doubting his forecast for their lives, Dr. Fuquan calm-ly asked, "What would you - each of you - consider vital in order to have a life worth living ... a life like the one you want to live?"

"Love," Maybeth spoke first after a brief lull. "I can't imagine life without it, and I want to find love again, or I will feel lonely and sad. That' s no way to live." Dr. Fuquan wrote LOVE in big letters on the board. "Health," Brian said. "What would it benefit us to live if we weren't healthy? Taking care of yourself - that's what makes my life worth living." HEALTH was added below LOVE. "Fulfillment," Carla added. "You know - like having a goal where you do something bigger than yourself ... or a job you really like something that fulfills you - makes you feel good about who you are." Dr. Fuquan silently wrote FULFILLMENT below the other words. "I am thinking ... some fun!" Wayne snickered as he said it. no one else laughed, he stammered, "Like vacations ... and ... and fun time you work for ... or hobbies ... you know, things like that." FUN joined the list on the board.

"Jennifer, Kevin?" Dr. Fuquan asked, glancing at each Person, offering them the opportunity to contribute. "Um." Jennifer spoke softly. "This may sound weird, but for me - I would say ... a family." Several others nodded. Emboldened, Jennifer explained, "Having children you can teach and who will carry on your name. That ... that's my ideal of happiness " After, Dr - Fuquan wrote FAMILY, everyone looked at Kevin. He shrugged. "Making sure you don't get abused - not letting anyone take advantage of you - being strong." Dr. Fuquan-nodded slowly. "And what does being strong mean to you, Kevin? Is it strictly a physical attribute?" Kevin moved his head up and down slowly then a furrow dug its way into his forehead, and the nodding stopped.

'"No... I mean physically strong is important but, well take my grandma before she died. She was the strongest person I knew, and maybe the weakest - physically, because of her illness." "How was she strong, Kevin?" His eyes glazed slightly, Kevin took a deep breath then said, "She was dying. -- I mean she knew it, everyone knew it. Her life was ending forever - but she never stopped smiling - never stopped trying to make others feel better. She said she knew where she was going, and that knowledge made her feel peace and happiness. I ... I wish I had that knowledge." The room was as quiet as a nun's bedroom. "What do you think was her source of that strength and knowledge?" Dr. Fuquan asked, a dignified reverence in his voice. Kevin thought a moment - the class barely breathing ... waiting. "Faith," he finally answered. "That woman had more faith than anyone I ever met. That's what made her strong."

Dr. Fuquan wrote FAITH at the end of the list, then turning back to the class, he said, "Take a look at your list. This is the list YOU compiled. Not me. LOVE - HEALTH - FULFILL-MENT - FUN - FAMILY - FAITH. How important are each of these? Could you say you had a complete life - one worth living - if we erased one of them ... and if so, which one?" Everyone stared at the board like it was a genie offering them three wishes. Dr. Fuquan waited patiently. "Gotta have 'em all," Brian spoke first. "I agree," Maybeth quickly agreed. "If you erase any one of them, your life is incomplete." Gradually every head was nodding in agreement.

Dr. Fuquan moved back behind the table. He pulled the paper face mask over his nose and mouth, then picked up a pair of surgical tongs. "Tonight," he announced, "we are going to amputate - extract - cut out - those attributes in each of you that prevent you from obtaining that happiness and success you desire ... and deserve. The characteristics that hinder your ability to reach the potential you were meant to achieve. Then, after the surgery, as is customary in such procedures, you will be given a prescription .. medicine to daily keep your arteries of happiness free from any clogs. Are you ready to begin?"

Anxiously, each answered affirmatively. Dr. Fuquan raised only a small section of the sheet. Using the tongs, he carefully probed around in the cadaver on the table, exaggerating his moves before finally clamping down on something. "Got it," he calmly said, and pulled from beneath the sheet a small poster board sign that read REVENGE. "The first obstruction we have encountered is revenge. This was difficult to remove because so many feel like it is necessary for then to live, and they have had it infesting their systems for so long, they have grown accustomed to it. But, as long as it remained inside, nothing pertaining to happiness could flow through you. This Must be extracted - and never allowed to grow its poisonous tentacles again." "Just like that?" Wayne scoffed. "Pull out a stupid piece of paper and revenge is gone? You really think it works like that?"

"Who puts your pants on for you, Mr. Wade?" Dr. Fuquan quickly asked, ignoring his comment. Wayne grimaced. "What? Nobody puts my pants on me. I put my own pants on every day," The irritation in his voice was obvious. "Of course, you do," the instructor confirmed. "Just as you also put on your own shoes or decide which TV show to watch ... or what kind of food you'll eat tonight. YOU, Mr. Wade, YOU make the decisions in your life. So why would you think you cannot make this decision, too? Why would you let me - or Carla .. or some priest at summer camp make the decision for you?" The doctor's eyes never wavered from Wayne's, even when the young man stiffened and clenched his fists. "And" Dr. Fuquan -- said sternly, "you make the decision to give up revenge."

But let me warn you, if you decide to hold on to it, if you opt to keep that revenge fresh in your mind - you are relinquishing your power giving your control and your decisions about your own happiness, to whoever it is you want to punish. They are now controlling you ... making your decisions for you. Is that what you want?" "NO! " Wayne nearly shouted. "Nobody will ever control me again!" "Then revenge has to go," Dr. Fuquan said, and he opened the tongs, letting the card drop into the waste basket.

"Next," he smoothly continued, sliding the tongs under the sheet again, "is .. " He dug around a minute while the class watched very intently, finally pulling out another card. This one had HATRED written on it. "Hatred," the doctor held up the card - holding it away from his body like it was toxic. "Hatred is just as life threatening as revenge." He walked around the table, holding the card at arm's length. "What do we hate .... why do we hate?" he asked. "Lots of reasons," Kevin answered. "Other people make you hate. People who are prejudice ... bigots, racists." "Bad drivers," Maybeth giggled. "I hate them!" "Stupid people," Carla rolled her eyes. "They don't even try to learn anything. They waste their lives and only stay around so they can mess up your life." "How about slobs?" Jennifer asked. "I hate those people who go into a restroom or a restaurant ... or anywhere and can't clean up after themselves."

Dr. Fuquan listened to the chatter for a few moments, then held up his hand. "Excuse me," he looked directly at Carla, "Ms. Warfield, earlier you said you hated everyone in this class. Why do you hate them?" Carla felt her face get hot. "I ... uh ... I guess I don't so much feel that way ... not so much ... anymore." Her chin seemed to be sewn to her chest. When Carla didn't speak further, Dr. Fuquan did. "If I may, let me suggest the reason for your hatred, and for your apparent change of attitude now." Without waiting for her permission, he continued. "You hated what you did not know - much like a child hates broccoli though he has never tried it. But once he samples it, many find out they really like it. You've come to know and interact with your classmates here, and the hatred has diminished with the level of your understanding and knowledge of who they are." "Yeah," Carla mumbled. "I guess so."

Looking at the class again, Dr. Fuquan said, "If hatred takes hold in your life, even a tiny root burrows in - your chance at happiness - lasting happiness - is dead." He dropped the card into the trash. "One more," he told the subdued class. "Anyone guess what it is?" "Anger!" almost all of them said at once. Dr, Fuquan smiled, reached under the sheet, and plucked out the third card. "The reason you are here," he said, holding up the word ANGER. "It is a terrible trait, but usually a byproduct of the other two." He swiftly opened the tongs and the card tumbled in with the others.

After a discussion on the perils of anger and its causes, and a review of how fatal all three attributes were, Dr. Fuquan held up a large poster that had been leaning against the wall. "As I promised," he said," I have the medicine you'll need to take at least 10 times each day in order to make sure those killers are eradicated from your life. Call it an antidote." He turned the board around. On it, in big block letters, was printed:

THERE IS NO CHANCE,

NO FATE, NO DESTINY THAT CAN CIRCUMVENT,

HINDER OR CONTROL,

THE FIRM RESOLVE - OF A DETERMINED SOUL!

"What?" Brian screwed up his face as he read the words. "What's it mean?" asked Wayne, equally perplexed. Carla had cold, hard eyes. "It means we determine our own fate, and nothing can stop us if we commit ourselves ... in our souls." "Excellent, Ms. Warfield," the Dr. said. "You are precisely accurate - both in your analysis and your interpretation." He propped the sign between the desk and the podium. "Let's briefly consider each part. Chance - in this venue - would mean luck I'll call it happenstance." He pointed at the word. "No chance - no accidental occurrence can deviate us. Just as no fate or predesigned destiny, can alter our course. We can't use those excuses if we fail. The failure comes from within us - and us alone. No more blaming - no more pity party - no more making excuses. No more crutches for our souls. Any idea what those crutches would be? The crutches that afflict our souls with a malady that steals our happiness." "Hatred, revenge and anger," the class responded like a choir. "Circumvent," the doctor tapped the word on the sign. "In this quote it connotes deception - our own deception of ourselves – a self-imposed roadblock or unexpected obstacle that internally tells us that we cannot attain the goal we have set. Here we are saying that we no longer accept those crutches and excuses NOTHING can circumvent or hinder or control our established goals if ... " he annunciated the final word louder, then paused "If we have a firm soul," Maybeth said. "A firm resolve in our soul." Dr. Fuquan merely nodded.

After the class quoted the adage aloud several times, Dr. Fuquan concluded his lesson. "I expect each of you to commit this to memory immediately, and to quote it a minimum of 10 times a day. This – just as with any other medication - is only effective when taken as prescribed. Only the patient knows if he or she has complied with the doctor's orders. But the patient seeking to become well - and to reach the happiness you each said you desired," he thumped the blackboard with his knuckle, drawing their attention back to their six words, "then you will do as instructed - and we'll talk about it when we meet again." As if late for a bus, Dr. Fuquan snatched up his dummy and exited the room - still wearing his hospital scrubs.

"James," Clay Stephenson greeted his old friend, "thank you for taking the time to meet me. I know it's an inconvenience" "Out of my way, yes, " Dr. Fuquan smiled, "but an inconvenience it is not. It is always a blessing to get to share some time with you. You worried about how I'm handling the class?" Clay cocked an eyebrow, "Psychologists are sworn to tell the truth?" He said, "I wasn't concerned about the class until I heard that little patronizing speech of yours." Both men smiled and took a seat in the office. "I am certainly not concerned about the class, James said.

"It's Judge O'Brien. The old man wants to know how they're doing. I believe he's worried something like the Sam Thomas thing could happen again." "I don't see that," James told him. "Then again, I doubt we would have predicted Sam's behavior any better than Ms. Thacker did had we been leading the class." Stephenson nodded. "Just the same, though, he wants a report. What should I tell him?" Dr. Fuquan considered the question. "You know, Clay, I've presented the direction I want them to go - leading them, I hope, to a conclusion they will make for themselves. Amongst themselves - together. For that reason, I haven't stayed around to discuss every detail of what we cover. I leave as quick as I can, knowing they will talk things over after I leave. If they help each other - even guide each other to the only beneficial verdict - I believe it will be more lasting more permanent."

Stephenson pushed his glasses up on his nose. "That sounds risky, James." "Possibly, we'll find out soon enough." "You're not telling me," Dr. Stephenson looked over the rims of his glasses, "that you don't have a read on your students, are you?" "No," Dr. Fuquan chuckled softly, "I'm not saying that at all. I'm saying that - in my professional opinion - tremendous progress has occurred. However, the extent and permanence of their behavioral adjustment will not be assessable until the final project is complete. Dr. Stephenson stroked his hairy chin with his fingertips. "That is what I'll tell the old judge, then." He looked across at his dear friend. "That, and the fact that the best psychologist I know is handling the class."

James grinned. "What was that about the truth all the time?" "Nothing could be truer," clay responded. "But tell me, James, are there any concerns? Anyone you think is borderline?" Fuquan pondered, scratched his temple, twisted his mouth. "All of them." he honestly answered. "There are lingering issues concerns about people in their past and that bothers me." "You'll keep an eye on it?" "I already am," he responded.

Chapter Thirty-Three

Releasing the pain

A SLIGHT CHILL HUNG in the October night air as Dallas experienced the first signs of Autumn. Dr. Fuquan ran his finger down the smooth black surface of his grand piano and pondered the upcoming evening. He plucked his hat off the rack by the front door and slipped on his jacket. He had taken over the class because Clay Stephenson was a good friend - a great friend - and he wanted to help anyone he could when possible. What he never counted on was the feeling of closeness of kinship with the students. He had watched their attitudes slowly change from the typical martyr syndrome, where nothing is their fault, to a tentative acceptance of their role in their own futures. But was it enough? He wondered. "Four more classes," he sighed. "Four more chances."

James had never married - never had a fiancé or a steady girlfriend since Sarah. He was an only child, and his parents were deceased. These 6 students though he could barely comprehend it himself -- were as close to a family relation-ship as he had ever experienced in his adult life. He knew he would miss them when they moved on with their lives and put the class and their close encounter with incarceration behind them. James stepped out into the night air. "You're getting soft, Fuquan," he told himself. "Do your job and your education and your piano will always be there for you as your companions and your family. You don't need more than that." He pushed the button on his key fob and the lights of his Mercedes 420 SEL clicked on with a twirping sound. "And you're a liar, too," he said opening the door. "You're just like them. You want more."

Commerce Street in Dallas runs nearly the length of the city. Downtown is the home of large banks, boutique shops, high end stores and five star restaurants. Dr. Fuquan had instruct-ed the class members to meet him at the corner of Com-merce and Houston Street. at the appropriate time. "Gonna spring for dinner at Morton's?" Brian asked him with a grin when the announcement was made. Dr. Fuquan returned the smile. "Don't be late ... and bring a jacket." James parked a few blocks away and walked, hoping the others would arrive before him. He was pleased to see all 6 of them hunched together on the corner as he approached. Kevin spotted him first. Glancing at his watch, he said, "Yer 3 minutes late, Doc.

Guess something circumvented or hindered or controlled your arrival time." "Or he wasn't a determined soul," Carla joked and nodded at him. Their reference to the proverb caused a flutter of satisfaction inside him.

"Thank you for being punctual, " the doctor said, "We have a lot to do. Everyone ready?" He really wanted to hug each one and tell them how amazing they were and how much he appreciated them. Maybe on the last day - when he handed them their certificates. For more than an hour the small band of classmates and their teacher peered in the windows of expensive stores, looked at price tags that seemed exorbitant, watched the crowds pass by - even looked at license plates and identified vehicles from 27 different states. Dr. Fuquan peppered them with question as they meandered through the streets.

"Why are all these people here? Why do they come to Dallas? Why is our city so popular and so loved? What causes people to want to spend their money here? Why are there so many jobs in Dallas when the country is suffering so much? How can the merchants get away with overpricing their goods?" The answers came from everyone. "Dallas is beautiful." "Our weather is great." "Our economy is good." "Rich people spend more money." "Tourists don't mind parting with their vaca-tion money."

Finally came the answer he was waiting for. "Dallas has a reputation as a great city," Jennifer said, and everyone verbally agreed with her. "None better than the Big D," Wayne said. "The Cowboys are America's team," Brian added. Dr. Fuquan smiled. "Ready for a short walk?" "You're the leader, Doc " Wayne marched up behind him. "Lead the way." Dr. Fuquan led them down Commerce St., walking silently and rapidly. He could hear the speedy click of heels behind him as the girls struggled to keep up. A few minutes later they reached the edge of Dealey Plaza. The doctor stopped, allowing the others to catch up. When everyone was rested, he asked, "We all know what happened here, don't we?" Somberly they nodded. "JFK was shot," Maybeth answered for the group. "November 22, 1963."

Letting a car pass, Dr. Fuquan stepped into the street a few paces. "It was right here," he said, standing directly in the middle of the road." The limo was right here when the fatal bullet tore through the President's head." No one made a sound. As a car slowed, flashing its lights at him, Dr. Fuquan strode back to the curb. But he didn't stop there. He kept walking - up the hill to the infamous grassy knoll. Like robots, the students fell in behind him, marching up the slope silently. Dr. Fuquan stopped at the top. "Turn around," he instructed. "Gaze out over our beautiful city - take a look at the 'Belle of Texas' - the Big D - the most amazing city in the world. Your city!"

The students did as he asked, rotating so they could observe the galaxy of twinkling lights below and around them. It appeared as though they were gazing at heaven - upside down. Each one reverently peered at the breathtaking, manmade aura stretching out as far as they could see. "Dallas was the most hated city in the world," the doctor explained. "This city had just murdered the President of the United States. City officials received death threats. Corporations cancelled their conventions. Dallas could have returned the hatred - Dallas could have sought revenge against those who blamed a city for solitary acts - Dallas could have withdrawn into a shell and remained angry at the world." He let his words hang in the air a moment, then went on. "But Dallas chose to focus on its future not its past. Dallas chose to define itself by the good it had - ignoring the opinions of those who chose to hate. And look at Dallas today. "

More silence. More respectful gazing. Jennifer interrupted the quiet. "We're like Dallas, aren't we? We can choose to hang on to the past and hate ... choose to be labeled by the mistakes we made, or we can move forward and create our own brilliance." "Because we all have a lot of good in us." Maybeth said. Dr. Fuquan spoke softly. "That's correct and how do we know we can do it? How do we know we can rise above our past and become anything we want to be?" Carla started it, but soon everyone was reciting along with her: There is no chance, no fate, no destiny, that can circumvent, or hinder or control, the firm resolve of a determined soul.

Chapter Thirty-Four

My hero

THE GROUP DISBURSED FROM Dealey Plaza - some in pairs, some alone. A few left on the bus, a couple walking towards their cars. Dr. Fuquan offered the last ones - Carla and Kevin- a ride. Both declined. Kevin wanted to visit a friend who lived in the area. Carla had arrived on foot - a 14-block walk from her apartment. She chose to walk home alone - unwilling to expose her humble conditions. Ten blocks from Dealey Plaza - the bright lights of downtown far behind her - Carla was walking leisurely, pondering the lessons of the evening. From the shadow in an alley, a figure slipped behind her, quietly closing the distance between them. Carla was so engrossed in her thoughts and her plans, her commitments to the future, that she wouldn't have heard the footsteps had they been loud. The soft, almost silent paces - were obscured even more by the traffic on the busy street a block to the south. Suddenly, directly in front of her, another figure emerged from the dark recesses of a building. Planting his feet firmly on the sidewalk, he grinned like a lottery winner.

Carla gasped and the other figure pulled up. "Hello, sis," Ricky said. He was older and bigger, but there was no mistaking him. Carla's nightmare had come true. She pivoted to run from him when the figure behind her grabbed her in a bear hug. The massive arms swallowed her up. Her heart pounded in her chest. "Where you been?" Donny chuckled. "Me and Ricky been looking for ya!" We been missin' our brotherly benefits. Carla struggled but Donny was far too strong. "Yeah," Ricky giggled. "We been looking for ya."

Unable to speak, barely able to breathe, Carla felt the fear rush through her entire body, panic gripping her like a vice. Her breath came out in short, halting pants. "My, my," Donny said, running his hands over her chest, "our little sister has become quite a woman. I think we're gonna like this a lot more now, Ricky." "Let me feel 'em ," Ricky gargled. "I wanna see 'em, too." Donny held her tight with one arm, using the other hand to clutch take nape of her blouse. With a vicious yank, he tore the material down the middle sending buttons flying as the garment sagged open. Ricky's hand clasped onto her breast, squeezing it brutally. "Yeah," he shouted. "Get the bra off, too, Donny." "Let's get her in the alley first," the older brother said. "Then the bra and everything else comes off." While Ricky snorted, Donny drug the frightened young woman towards the darkness.

Just as they reached the entrance to the alley, a voice from the darkness said, "Let the girl go!" Donny and Ricky both squinted to see who was talking. No one was visible. "Let the girl go!" the voice repeated. Donny clutched tighter. "I don't think so!" he snarled. "And whoever you are, I suggest you get out of here right now, or you'll end up a lot worse than the girl." "Yeah," Ricky cowered behind his brother. "She's our sister. We'll do whatever we want to with her." In the eerie blackness of the alley, the brothers could see a figure aggressively moving towards them. Donny pitched Carla to the pavement, her body crashing hard onto the surface, her head cracking against the asphalt, her knees and elbows scraping hard and drawing blood.

"Come on, Ricky," Donny shouted. "Let's take care of this punk." Donny pulled a knife from his pocket while Ricky yanked a Saturday night special from his waistband, his hand shaking as he fumbled to get a secure grip on the pistol. Donny raised the knife and lunged at the shadowy figure. As if he were a ghost, the unknown man was gone - sending Donny stumbling through the empty space. Before he could steady his feet again, a hand shot forward, snatching the gun from

Ricky's fingers and, in a fluid motion, landed a crushing blow on the younger man's nose. The sound of cracking bone and Ricky's body thumping hard on the road brought Donny spinning around. Angrily, he clutched the knife tighter and rushed at the man for a second attempt.

Hardly moving, the man easily dodged Donny. He grabbed the wrist that held the knife and shoved him forward causing Donny to drop the weapon. Donny immediately turned, a hint of fear crossing his face. He swore loudly, then opened his arms wide and rushed a third time, corralling the man and wrestling him to the ground. They struggled for a moment before Donny was overpowered. The man pinned Donny's arm under his knees and begin throwing punches knocking Donny unconscious. Before leaving the man stomped Donny's head three times with the heel of his boot.

Carla had been watching through blurred vision. She was still lying prone on the asphalt where Donny had thrown her, blood oozing from a gash on her head. Too discombobulated to even stand up or flee, she was struggling to clear her vision to see who was beating up Donny and Ricky - who had rescued her. Squinting in the inky darkness, she could see only his back. When Donny fell to the ground, Carla looked up as the man turned to her. Gasping audibly, she whispered, "Dr. Fuquan...""

Chapter Thirty-Five

A close watch

D R. FUQUAN GENTLY PICKED Carla up from the pavement and cradled her in his arms. He carried her back to his car, laying her on the reclined front seat. She drifted in and out of consciousness while he sped across town to Parkland Hospital, shaking slightly as he realized how close he had come to missing the attack. "All those nights following her," he muttered, swerving around the slower traffic, "and they came at her while I was parking the car." Shortly after accepting the assignment to lead the anger management class, Dr. Fuquan had covertly canvassed each student's home and neighborhood, seeking a better understanding of who he'd be teaching. In Carla's file, next to her address and other pertinent information, was a description of the horrible atrocities that had occurred at the hands of her adopted brothers. His heart ached for the frail youngster staring back at him in the photograph.

When Dr. Fuquan turned the page, clipped to the back of the file folder was a picture of the Warfield family. Looking into the eyes of the two brothers - Donny and Ricky - James saw a familiar sign in their eyes evil. Returning to his home one night, a week after taking over the class, the doctor saw two men lurking on a corner just 3 blocks from the school. Instantly he recognized them Donny and Ricky Warfield. He circled the block and watched from a distance as Carla strolled carefree down the street. She followed a route that took her a block north of the spot where Donny and Ricky had been standing, and arrived safely at her apartment, Dr. Fuquan followed in his car easing slowly a hundred yards behind her all the way. He knew, however, that it was only a matter of time before the brothers spotted her. They had obviously heard she was in the area and were looking for her.

Every class thereafter Dr. Fuquan - keeping a safe distance to avoid detection - had shadowed Carla on her walks back to her home. He had waited in the diner behind the menu the night she and Wayne visited - and was her guardian angel until she was in her house, and he heard the sound of the latch on the door snapping locked. Then he took a cursory lap or two around the block, just to make sure no one was trying to get at her. This night, after watching her walk away from Dealey Plaza, he had retrieved his car and hurried up the road, trying to catch up to her. When he saw Ricky duck into an alley and Donny lurking a block behind, he parked his car and approached - through the alley - on foot. And just in time!

"Are you a relative?" the nurse at Parkland asked when Dr. Fuquan brought Carla through the electronic doors. "I know her," he answered. "I'm her teacher. I witnessed the attack." The nurse nodded and immediately took charge. Carla was placed on a gurney and rushed to an exam room while Dr. Fuquan gave a statement to the police. "You'll find her attackers in the alley," he said, giving them the address. "I believe they were struck by a vehicle. or something very powerful - maybe while assaulting the young lady. I just picked her up and hurried here. I didn't check on them. A patrol car was dispatched to pick up the Warfield boys and Dr. Fuquan followed the nurse, who led him to the room where Carla was being treated. "She'll be admitted," the nurse said. "She has a severe concussion, and the doctor is concerned there may be swelling on the brain."

Chapter Thirty-Six

Making a new Family

B RIAN BROUGHT BALLOONS - dozens of balloons! Maybeth snuck a large platter of homemade cookies past the nurse's station. Jennifer created a huge GET-WELL poster that everyone signed, along with motivational encouragement. Kevin arrived with a menagerie - more than a dozen stuffed animals. Wayne brought a T-shirt - DKNY brand - with six simple words stenciled on it: WE'RE FAMILY AND WE LOVE YOU. Each class member had signed the shirt with a Sharpie. Wayne also brought a tear – actually, several of them. Had Carla's condition remained serious, Dr. Fuquan would not have suggested they meet at the hospital instead of the classroom. The attending physician told him she was out of danger but needed to remain in the hospital a few more days for observation and testing. "I... I ... can't believe this!"

Carla choked back tears of her own wiping a sniffle from her nose. "Oh, honey," Maybeth sang in her Dallas drawl, "you might still hate us, but we love you. Don't we?" She turned to the others who nodded and verbally agreed with her. "I... I don't hate you." Carla whimpered, her heart "I ... you are ... you're the closest I've ever had to ... to a family." "And we always will be," Jennifer leaned over the low rail and hugged her. With cookies crumbling, Carla reading the messages on the card, and Dr. Fuquan monitoring the door - keeping a lookout for any 'Nurse Hatchett' who might frown on their little party.

The lesson was hard to deliver, but the doctor tried. "Carla's attackers have been incarcerated ... or ... they will be," he explained, "when they are released from the hospital." "How'd you get away?" Brian asked Carla. "And what happened to them? They were really messed up - from what I heard." Honoring Dr. Fuquan's request, Carla shrugged. "I heard someone told the police they were possibly hit by a passing car." "Wow!" Maybeth shook her head. "God sent that car down that street. Carla knew God had sent something down the street that night, and it took all she had not to reveal her true guardian angel.

It had taken her awhile just to recreate the evening - the attack, the voice from the alley, the crash on the pavement when Donny threw her down, and the hazy, blurry vision of Dr. Fuquan as he methodically and easily dispatched the two thugs with such finesse. "You haven't always been a psychologist, were you?" Carla had asked him the next day when her mind was beginning to clear. "We all have a past." Dr. Fuquan responded, avoided the question. "I am no different than you. I, too, needed someone to reach out and scrape me from the road metaphorically." "You were attacked?" Carla gasped. James Fuquan smiled. "Metaphorically," he repeated louder. "I was rescued from my life of hatred and anger and revenge just as surely as you were raised from the pavement. Only," he paused and swallowed hard, "My predicament was much more lethal than your condition. You were physically hurt - I was psychologically impaired and that was sure to be fatal for me and for anyone around me."

"You learned the poem, right?" Carla naively asked Dr. Fuquan laughed softly, his smile wide, his brown eyes sparkling with pride. "The poem ... and a lot more. I needed a lot more, but the poem was important." "Why didn't you tell us?" she wrinkled her forehead. "Some of us were thinking you were a rich kid - never had a problem in your entire life. If we had known." Dr. Fuquan interrupted her. "The change each of you must make has to be internal. If you change because someone else did, it's temporary. You need to find the solutions and determine the path for yourself."

"But we couldn't do it without you." another smile. "I'll take credit for providing you all with the opportunity to change but it was you - and the rest of the class - who do the heavy lifting and make the change a permanent part of your life." Carla creased her forehead a moment. "So," she asked, " what is the secret then? I mean, after all we've learned, what did you do to get us to make the right choices?" Dr. Fuquan pulled the blanket up as if he were tucking her in bed for the night. "I taught you correct principles," he said softly, "and let you govern yourselves. That's the only way a person can make the change and alter his or her life." Carla pondered that as sleep crept over her. Before she drifted off, Dr. Fuquan had her promise that the secret was theirs alone. "The class needs to make their own conclusions and choose the life they want." he said. "Promise me you'll let them do that." "I promise," Carla's groggy voice whispered.

And she was keeping that promise now. Amid the barrage of questions from the others, Carla snuck a peek at Dr. Fuquan, who quietly kept vigil near the door, attempting to draw their attention to present the lesson, knowing they were celebrating and that the closeness they were experiencing right now was more powerful than any words he could utter. Watching and listening carefully, Dr. Fuquan detected an anger brewing inside Wayne. "If those guys live," Wayne swore, "I'll finish the job the car started." The others joked and took his words as part of the banter, but Dr. Fuquan could see it the anger was still there. "No, you won't"

Carla grabbed his arm and pulled him close. "You're not gonna go and mess up your life for them. Just when I' m starting to think a white boy might not be so bad." She pulled him down and kissed him on the cheek, much to the delight of the rest of the class. "But," she added, still holding onto him, "thank you for your gallantry. It means a lot to me." The evening was perfect. "Our final class," Dr. Fuquan told them, "Will be a small party and a short lesson. As soon as Carla is able to attend,"

"We love you, sweetheart," Maybeth said again as she left the hospital room. "Get well, Carla," Jennifer told her. Kevin's voice echoed through the room, "See you in class." "No chance, no fate." "Ok, Brian," the others poked him and chided him while Carla grimaced from a laugh that made her head hurt. "Thank you for coming!" she said a hundred times as they filed out. "I'll be well, soon. " The door closed, and Carla looked up. Wayne was still standing in the room. He walked slowly to her bedside. Carla saw the concern on his face. Was it fear? Was he worried she would never recover? "What is it,

Wayne?" she asked. "Something is bothering you. I'm going to be fine; you know. So, what is it?"

"I found him," Wayne whispered. Carla's smile evaporated. She instantly knew who Wayne had found. In their partnership chats Wayne had - reluctantly - told her some of his secrets, divulging some of the sordid details of what happened in his youth ... at the summer camp. "You're the only one in the class who knows what happened to me," Wayne kept whispering. "And so, you know how much I hate that guy - and how much he deserves what happens to him." His features were taut, his eyes glazed, almost demonic. "Father Murphy," Carla eked out the name in short syllables. "He's the Priest at a Diocese in Ft. Worth,"

Wayne's breathing was deeper. "He's probably doing the same thing to boys there." "Wayne," Carla grabbed his arm so hard her fingernails dug into his flesh. "Don't you go there." She was near tears as she pleaded with him. "Let it go. Bury the revenge. Remember what Dr. Fuquan..." "To hell with Dr. Fuquan..." Wayne growled through clenched teeth. "That prissy prick. He's no man. You saw how he wimped off in the corner tonight. Embarrassed he had no answers for what happened to you. His little speeches don't mean shit in real life. All his fancy talk - sure didn't protect you, did it? He's just a bag of words. He doesn't care about us." "He does," Carla moaned, her face streaked with tears, her heart and her head battling - She had given her word to Dr. Fuquan, yet she felt she needed to reach out to Wayne - to save him from a disaster he was about to create.

"He does care," she repeated. "He sees us as a payday, and that's it!" Wayne's voice was loud and strong now - angry. "No," Carla shook her head, "he ... he is." "He is what?" Wayne snapped at her. "What is he?" "He - Dr. Fuquan ... he's the one," she felt tears gush from her eyes as she told him. Wayne was confused. "The one? What are you talking about?" Carla was nearly sobbing. "There was no car, Wayne. Donny and Ricky weren't struck by a car ... they ..." She took a deep breath, trying to control her emotions and her voice. Wayne's face was distorted in confusion. "Dr. Fuquan," Carla said, as evenly as she could, "he didn't just find me, Wayne. He saved me. He beat up Donny and Ricky. He stopped them from attacking me. He saved my life!"

Wayne blinked several times. He was at a loss for words. If Carla was telling him the truth then everything he thought about Dr. Fuquan ... all he clung to in order to justify holding on to his hatred and his plans for revenge, were shattered. Dr. Fuquan wasn't a wimpy scholar reciting mantras for a fee. He was a concerned friend. "Not true!" Wayne shook his head. "Not true!" "Yes," Carla bawled. "It is. He ... he's followed me for weeks. He saw Donny and Ricky casing the area and knew they 'd try something. He ... he felt bad he got there late and had to handle the situation with violence, but." "I got to go," Wayne cut her off, turned sharply, his mind rushing with conflicting thoughts "Wayne!" Carla called out, begging. "Don't." The door closed with a loud thunk!

Chapter Thirty-Seven

Patience is a virtue

"**T**HIS IS OUR LAST class together," Dr. Fuquan softly announced when the group had all arrived. Carla had been hugged and patted and congratulated on her recovery so many times she began to imagine this was what life could really be like - support ... concern ... care ... love... family. "Don't forget the dinner you promised," Maybeth reminded him of the Thanksgiving plans they had made during one of their group visits to the hospital. "The Court said I can pick up Ashley for the weekend!" she beamed. "We want to spend it with you guys ... you're our family now."

Dr. Fuquan smiled. "I haven't forgotten. My house - Thanksgiving Day. I even have directions printed off for each of you." He passed around the papers with the map to his home. "You are doing the cooking, Doc?" Brian asked. "What can we bring?" Maybeth wanted to know. The Dr. looked directly at her. "For most of you, just bring yourselves. That will be a treat for me. But ... " he raised his eyebrows in expectation, "I was hoping I could convince you, Mrs. Simmons, to come over the day before. I'm a master chef when it comes to rib eyes, but I'm not willing to subject all of you to a turkey I cooked, since I've never cooked one before." "Oh!" Maybeth giggled with delight, "I'd love to ... oh ... can I bring Ashley?' "It's a requirement," the Dr. joked. "And I'll let you decide the rest of the menu as well." The suggestions and demands flowed fast and instantly. "Stuffing," Kevin said. "Good stuffing, with giblets and gravy." Brian rubbed his stomach. "Got to be mashed potatoes or it's not really Thanksgiving!"

"And candied yams," Jennifer gleamed as she thought of them. "Ain't comin' unless you got pumpkin pie," Wayne tried to sound tough. Carla, sitting across the aisle from Wayne, stroked his arm. "I'm not coming." She corrected him. "Ain't ... has to go!" "Oh, yeah," Wayne half smiled. "She thinks she's gonna make me a linguistical guy." The class chuckled, and Carla smiled. Wayne shrugged. "It's pumpkin pie, right?" Maybeth was giggling like a schoolgirl. "There will be pumpkin pie ... I promise." Dr. Fuquan brought the class back to their reason for meeting "Tonight," he said, "since Carla is back with us ... I thought a cake would be appropriate."

"OK! " Kevin nearly shouted. "Now we're talkin'!" Dr -Fuquan produced three round pans, each covered with tin foil. He placed them on the table at the front of the room, then brought out three cans of frosting and six kitchen knives, laying them on a napkin at the side. "I brought the cakes, but didn't get them frosted," he said as he motioned to the items on the table. "So, rather than just frost them, I decided we would have a little fun competition. You up for it?" "If it means eating cake, then hell yes!" Brian licked his lips for emphasis. "OK," the doctor stood behind the table. "Here's how we'll do it. In pairs - your partnership pairs – you'll rush to the table, one twosome at a time, when I give you the signal. I'll start my stopwatch. You take off the foil, open the frosting, and ice your cake as fast as you can, then, we will all judge your performance, on a scale of 1 - 10. You'll get one second off your time for each point awarded you on your neatness. A 7 for example, would reduce your score by 7 seconds. So, speed and neatness are both important. Everybody got it?"

"Yeah, yeah," they nodded, agreeing. "Then let's get started," he said, moving one cake, one can of frosting, and two knives to the center of the table. "How about Carla and Wayne - you two go first." They smiled, gave a high 5, and indicated they were ready. Dr. Fuquan said "GO!" and hit the start button on his watch. Carla and Wayne rushed the table. Wayne tore open the frosting while Carla removed the foil cover-ing the cake. They each grabbed a knife and, clinking them together, fighting for speed, giggling and smearing - frosting everywhere - they splattered the cake ... and the table - finally announcing "FINISHED!"

Dr. Fuquan stopped his watch and wrote, "27.6 seconds" on the board. Laughter broke out when the cake was displayed. Globs of frosting hung on the sides of the pan, and swirls and deep grooves were all over the top of the cake. Suggested neatness points ranged from 2 - 6. "We'll give them a 5," Dr. Fuquan decided, and changed their score to "22.6 seconds," "Next Kevin and Mrs. Simmons," "It's Maybeth," she said for the hundredth time since the class had begun. "Maybeth," Dr Fuquan nodded, using her first name for the first time since the class had begun. "Thank you," she nodded. "I'm so tired of you calling me by HIS name. Only took three months to get you to call me Maybeth." "Ready?" the Dr. asked, eyeing his stopwatch. "Go!"

When Maybeth removed the foil and Kevin opened the icing, it was obvious they had discussed a plan. Alternating turns, they efficiently frosted the cake, without hurrying, in 20.4 seconds. It was presented to the class, and a consensus gave them a 10. Dr. Ferguson adjusted their time to 10.4 seconds. Maybeth bowed deeply while Kevin stuck his finger in the remaining icing ang licked it off. "That's going to be a tough score to beat," Dr. Fuquan observed, looking at the board. "NO problem," Brian boasted, holding hands with Jennifer. When Dr. Fuquan clicked his watch, Brian and Jennifer moved swiftly to the front, Brian was tearing open the last can of frosting when Jen yanked off the foil. They both stopped, like they had run into a wall. They stared for a second at the pan. "WAIT!" Jennifer exclaimed. "This ... this isn't baked!" She tipped the pan and the cake batter oozed to one side. "It's raw!" "Better hurry," Dr. Fuquan said, still looking at his watch. "You're wasting time."

"But we can't" "Come on!" Brian spouted, digging into the icing and globing a blob onto the gooey mixture. "Uck!" Jennifer screwed up her face, watching him, then lopped a hunk of frosting in with it. They both tried to spread the icing, but their knives became coated with the mixture of batter and icing. The class was laughing loudly, watching their frustration. After 47 seconds, they gave up - dropped the knives on the table and stared at their mess. Dr. Fuquan wrote 47.1 seconds on the board, then held up the gooey mess for observation. The laughter increased. "That wasn't fair," Jennifer insisted. Brian agreed. "It sure wasn't!" "Wait," Dr. Fuquan silenced the jovial attitude. "This cake is exactly like the other two -

exact same ingredients - 100%! I know because I made all 3 of them." "But this one isn't baked!"

Brian shot him an exasperated look. "Baked?" Dr. Fuquan feigned surprise. "But I'm going to bake it. Soon as you frosted it later, you know. Everything will be done ... just that this one will be baked a little later. Isn't that, OK?" "No! " Jennifer gave a little stomp with her foot. "You have to bake it FIRST BEFORE you put on the icing." "You do?" Dr. Fuquan acted naive. "Why?" Brian held up the pan. "This is why! It's ruined." "That really matters?" the Dr. creased his brow, "the order in which you do things?" "Of course, it does," Brian shook his head. "If you frost the cake before you bake it, the frosting will burn and the whole thing will be wasted," "I mean, just look at it." Jen was frowning at the cake mess. "OK, " Dr Fuquan took the cake pan from Brian. "Why don't you two have a seat?"

When Brian and Jennifer were in their desks, Dr. Fuquan, very serious now, asked the class, "Do we ever try to frost our cake before we bake it?" They each stared at him, realizing this had all been a lesson of some kind. "What do you mean?" Carla asked for the class. "In life," the doctor explained, "We see people frosting the cake before they bake it ... all the time. We see young marrieds who go into deep debt for furniture or trips or luxuries - before they have earned the money. They want their frosted cake, but they don't have the patience to wait until it's baked." The group was following him, hanging on every word.

"Or sexual relations," Dr. Fuquan ventured, "How many want the icing without baking the cake? Jennifer, you said this cake was ruined, but it's just a cake. However, when we jump around from icing to icing, and never bothering to bake a cake - never making a commitment to anyone, I'm here to tell you that you'll never taste how delicious the cake can be when it is baked first and then iced and you run the very serious risk of ruining the cake of others - your partners... children born to single parents. It's a dangerous game of Russian roulette we play when we do that. And why? Because we have been told that the icing is the best part. I'll admit, it is delicious, but the frosting is just a thin. layer. The cake is what we're preparing. And," he held up the pan one more time, "it's a mess - a ruined mess - if we think we can do things in the wrong order and still be happy. It's a lie we tell ourselves. And it's theft! A robbery of the happiness we could experience ... if we baked the cake before we frosted it."

The lesson was not lost. The class generated several more good examples of how people frost their cakes before baking them. From drug and alcohol abuse to gambling, they covered a myriad of topics, likening them to the cake and icing demonstration. When the class disbursed, leaving slowly, the discussion continued, along with plans to meet on Thursday, at Dr. Fuquan's house, for Thanksgiving dinner, where he would pass out their certificates for successfully completing the course. "And," Brian deadpanned, looking at Maybeth, "Be sure to bake that turkey before you frost it." as they laughed, Wayne said, "And the pumpkin pie, too."

Chapter Thirty-Eight

Justice prevails

THIS HAD BECOME THEIR routine, Brian walked Jennifer home after the class, discussing along the way the lesson Dr. Fuquan had taught them that particular night. They had barely covered half of the 10-block walk, chatting nonstop, when a car skidded around the corner out of control, and headed directly for them. Brian reacted instantly, throwing himself between Jennifer and the fast-approaching vehicle. With a hearty shove, he launched her out of the car's path and up on the lawn. At the same time, he dove for cover, turning a somersault like a gymnast and popping back to his feet in front of the startled Jennifer. The car bounced off the curb than wobbled away at a high speed. "Oh, my gosh!" Jennifer was holding on to Brian to steady herself. "I could have been hit!" Bryan just stared down at her, admiring her beautiful green eyes, He was wanting so badly to touch her, to hold her, to caress her, to comfort her. The silence extended as they gazed at each other.

When Jennifer spoke, her voice was soft, sensual and alluring. "You have become my best friend," she told him. "You're mine too," Brian awkwardly blurted out. For a star football player, with aspirations of a professional career he felt more intimidated by the little young woman in front of him than any linebacker he ever had run into. Jennifer's phone rang. It was Mrs. Singer, the dean's secretary at the college.

Jennifer: Hello?

Mrs. Singer: Jennifer Potter please.

Jennifer: This is she.

Mrs. Singer: Yes, Mrs. Potter. This is Mrs. Singer at the SMU administration office I'm calling to inform that our investigation regarding Kyle Weiser, and his frat brothers has been concluded. Mr. Weiser has been charged and arrested and escorted off campus. Indefinitely. We would like to invite you to return back to class after the holidays.

Jennifer: Will I be given an opportunity for make-up assignments I'm missing?

Mrs. Singer: Miss Potter that was discussed with some of the professors, and yes, you'll be given some additional assignments.

Jennifer: OK thank you. I'll see you on Monday.

With a big smile Jennifer shared the good news with Brian. "That's great! I'm so happy for you! We have to celebrate!" As he stood there, face-to-face, holding her hand. She searched his face and said "When Dr. Fuquan put us together as partners, I... I... Thought you were going to kiss me that night." Brian blinked nervously. "Why? I mean ... why would you think that?" He stammered. She tilted her head back a little. "Because I wanted you to." She whispered. Intimidated or not, Brian knew an invitation... one he dreamed about... fantasized about. Gently he lowered his head, his lips melting with hers and an undeniable explosion of satisfaction happened. They stayed there on an unknown lawn, locked together for several minutes. The curvaceous contours of her body pressing close to him. "You're coming home with me." Jennifer wasn't asking she was informing. When they finally separated, Brain said "We have been baking this cake long enough - it's time for some icing!"

Chapter Thirty-Nine

Regaining control

ASHLEY WAS READY AND waiting on Wednesday morning when Maybeth pulled up to the foster home where her daughter had been staying. Though she had been by to see her every day with promises that "we will be a family again soon," this was the first time the courts had approved an overnight stay - in fact, Maybeth was given permission to keep her through the long Thanksgiving weekend. "If this goes well," the magistrate had said in open court, "we will entertain a motion to return Ashley to your custody permanently." Maybeth couldn't hold back the tears of joy. "Thank you, Your Honor!" she sobbed. "Thank you so very much!" "The reports I've received have been favorable." the Judge told her. "You seem to have made significant progress. I don't think I have ever read a more glowing assessment before." "Reports?" Maybeth asked. "Who - who is reporting?"

Her head leaped when Judge O'Brien said, "A Dr. James Fuquan, your anger management instructor. I'm sure you are familiar with him?" "Oh, yes," Maybeth smiled wide behind her tear-streaked face. "I know Dr. Fuquan and," she dabbed her eyes with a tissue, "he happens to be the most amazing instructor I have ever had - in any subject." The judge returned her smile. "I'll note that in the record, Mrs. Simmons. Now, before we adjourn, I would like to ask you about your relationship with your husband."

Maybeth felt a stab of panic ... or anger! Was the judge testing her? Was he trying to see if she would get angry and vent at him and at Leon? As if a movie were playing in her mind, playing at triple speed, Maybeth instantly saw a pile of garbage dumped on her living room rug ... Dr. performing 'surgery' - extracting hate, anger and revenge ... the sparkling lights of an atoned Dallas shimmering before her ... a cake covered in beautiful, delicious frosting .. and she could almost taste the Dutch Apple pie that filled her vision. She looked at the Judge with a serene calmness.

She hadn't planned it, but the words tumbled out: "There is no chance, not fate, no destiny, that can circumvent, hinder or control, the firm resolve of a determined soul." The judge looked like a dog hearing a high-pitched whistle. "Pardon me," he said. Maybeth smiled. "My life is spread out before me like a trackless field of snow." she quoted Dr. Fuquan. "Since every step I take will leave a lasting imprint, I must remove certain influences before I begin my journey. Unfortunately, that means terminating a nearly 20-year relationship. But, for my welfare, and the safety of my precious daughter Ashley, I have filed for divorce."

"Are you sure you want to do that?" the judge looked down at her over the rims of his glasses. "Your Honor," Maybeth felt peace as she spoke, hearing Dr. Fuquan's voice in her mind as if he were standing next to her, coaching her. "A wound filled with poison and infection will never heal. New growth cannot occur in that environment. I am removing the poison and curing the infection, so Ashley and I can both heal, and begin to grow again."

The judge looked spellbound. "Mrs. Simmons," he said in hushed tones, "your speech is very eloquent, and your grasp of your situation and your life gives me great hope - belief even - that we will very soon be here again with a permanent order returning full parental custody to you." Maybeth spoke again. "Judge O'Brien, because of the circumstances and my behavior, I have not been able to appropriately mourn nor adequately comfort Ashley after the passing of my daughter - her sister. My heart's deepest desire is to raise a healthy, safe, well-adjusted child who contributes to the world in a positive manner." Judge O'Brien could just stare at her, admiring not only the progress she had made, but the strength of her convictions.

Maybeth could barely sleep Tuesday night. When Ashley came bounding out of the house with her overnight bag in hand, mother and daughter clutched each other like they had been apart for years. "I love you, Mommy," the little girl's words were the sweetest melody any mother could hear. In the car, Maybeth explained that they were not going straight home. "We're going to a friend's house," she said. "A good friend of mine. We're going to help him fix Thanksgiving dinner. Then, tomorrow, we're going back to help him eat it!" "Yeah!" Ashley shouted. "Can I make the Jell-o?" "You sure can, sweetheart," Maybeth hugged her as she strapped her into her car seat. "You can make the Jell-o 'cuz you've already made the happiness."

Chapter Forty

Does color really matter?

THE IMPRESSIVE REDWOOD SIGN announced the entrance to MANHATTAN ESTATES. The security building sat nestled between the thick 12-foot-tall hedges and the massive iron gate. Maybeth grinned as she rolled her car towards the uniformed guard whose white-gloved hand was held out in front of him. Maybeth had never visited London, but she imagined the bobby's standing at attention at Buckingham Palace were no more dignified in the performance of their duties than this young man at Manhattan Estates. "May I help you?" the sentry asked, leaning slightly to look in through Maybeth's open window. Almost giggling with excitement, Maybeth answered, "We're here to see Dr. James Fuquan. He's expecting us." Your names, Ma'am?" The voice was gentle but left no doubt who was in charge. "Maybeth," she answered politely, then added, "Simmons," in a less enthusiastic tone. "And my daughter, Ashely."

The guard returned to his full height with a trace of a grin, then pressed a button and the towering gates swung open exposing an Eden ... a Shangri-La of statuesque mansions and long, fertile lawns. "Dr. lives on ...” "Oh, I know," Maybeth smiled wide, showing him the map. "One left and two rights. We can find it. Thank you so much." "As you wish, Ma'am," the guard said, stepping aside to let her pass through. "Wow!" Ashley exclaimed, wide-eyed as Maybeth pulled into the driveway of the three-story brick, sprawling, mansion. "That's the biggest house I ever saw in my whole life." Maybeth laughed out loud, wondering how many houses a 5-year-old had seen. "This is Dr. Fuquan's house," she explained. "He is Mommy's friend. He helped me get well so we can be a family again." "I like Dr. Fu-can, Ashley cackled, waiting to be freed from her car seat."

Maybeth softly corrected her, Ashley parroted back the name correctly. The front door swung open like the portal of a wonderland. The doctor greeted them wearing a black V-neck fitted sweater. "Welcome to my home, you must be Ashley," he smiled, kneeling down to the child's level. Ashley nodded. "That's right, Dr. Fu-quan!" She half shouted the final syllable in triumph. "Well, come on in here, young lady," he scooped her into his arms. "We got ourselves a big old turkey that needs fixing up and cooked." "And you need Jell-o, too," Ashley slid her arms around his neck and hugged him. "Mommy said I can make it." "I suppose we do need that," he said, "And I'll bet you're the best Jell-o maker this house has ever seen." "I AM!" an emphatic Ashley told him. "'cept Mommy has to pour the water 'cuz it's so hot. But I do the stirring and that's the most important part."

When they entered the house Maybeth's eyes bulged. "This sure doesn't look like a bachelor pad," she noted, staring at the quality furniture - the paintings along the wall - the shelves of neatly lined books and the spacious rooms. The doctor shrugged. "Don't know a word for a male 'old maid' except 'bachelor', so I guess that's what I am. If Maybeth thought the living room was stimulating, the kitchen literally took her breath away. The wide granite counters glistened under the recessed lighting and the appliances sparkled. James sat Ashley on one of the stools facing the counter, then turned to see Maybeth standing in the doorway, her mouth gaped open.

"You, OK?" he asked. "It's - it's gorgeous!" Maybeth panted. "What a kitchen!!" "It came with the house." he shrugged shyly, "but I can say it has never looked better than it does right now." He felt clumsy trying to compliment her, but she smiled discreetly, then wrinkled her forehead. "Why?" her eyes were looking across from her- where two Sub Zero refrigerators were mounted in the wall, their front panels matching the rest of the cabinets, "why do you need 2 refrigerators?" Dr. chuckled. "Again, came with the house." Maybeth sighed. "I thought you were the world's heaviest beer drinker."

"I am not much of a beer drinker," the Dr. admitted, "but I do seem to find uses for both of them. Like now, the one on the left is filled with the ingredients I thought we would need to prepare tomorrow's dinner." Maybeth smiled so wide her cheeks ached. "Then let's get this show started." For the next several hours - interrupted only by a pizza lunch break Ashley's choice delivered from the local Papa John's store - the 3 of them peeled potatoes, laughed, chopped vegetables, told stories, prepared yams, spilled flour, tickled each other, told more stories, stuffed the turkey, and laughed and talked and laughed and talked some more and made definitely made Jell-o!

Ashley tired out around 2: 00 p.m. Dr. laid her on the bed in one of his guest rooms then coaxed Maybeth to take a break and enjoy a cup of tea with him. "This has to be the most fun I have ever had in my life," Maybeth held the cup in both hands, looking across the coffee table at the very relaxed psychologist. "Turns out you're quite the comedian and entertainer and cook. What other talents do you have that I should know about?" James studied her for a moment - her shimmering blond hair, her flawless complexion, her toned yet voluptuous body. "Well." he twisted his mouth as if he were thinking deeply, "you already know about my charisma and tremendous sex appeal, right?"

Maybeth giggled an infectious, contagious, joyful chorus he had not heard in his home ever! When she reached across the small table and touched his arm - gently laying her fingers on his forearm, electricity shot through him in a rush - a foreign sensation one he had calloused himself against - one he had hidden away behind his personal walls and past demons. "You are such a delight," Maybeth smiled, her soft, moist lips more alluring and enticing than any of the delicious dishes they had been preparing all day. Feeling his heart pounding, James rose to his feet. "We still have some pie crusts to make," he mumbled, a nasal nervousness enveloping him. Since the day he took over the anger management class, James had felt a connection with Maybeth Simmons. But - how could it be possible? Why would she be interested in him? Theirs was a professional relationship and he needed to act accordingly.

Maybeth made a pouting face, then stood up with him. "Back to the salt mines, eh, Dr.?" "It's James, I insist you call me James." He said, "outside of the classroom." "And NO

MORE MRS. SIMMONS!" Maybeth declared. "Besides, I'm taking my maiden name back as soon as the divorce is final." "Divorce?" James snapped his head around to look at her. "Duh?" Maybeth cracked. "You didn't think I was going to stay with that guy, did you?" "Uh .." James stammered, hopeful - his palms sweating. "No uh surely not, wouldn't, I mean not stay ... not you." Maybeth laughed. "Very eloquent for a renowned psychologist." James felt himself blush. Retreating to the kitchen, they resumed their preparations - and their laughing - and their talking - and their subtle flirting. Both were exhausted when they placed the final salads and other dishes into one of the refrigerators. "Enough food to feed my entire neighborhood," Maybeth said, wiping a drop of perspiration from her brow. "Should we invite them?" James joked.

Maybeth shook her head. "This is a family dinner - just family is invited. Besides, I think Brian and Kevin can clean up what the rest of us don't eat." James chuckled, noting her reference to family - to the class members being a family unit - gave James a warmth he enjoyed. Family had been a term others used - never him. Maybeth tossed her apron on the counter and marched out of the kitchen. "Time for my tour of the palace," she said, grabbing his arm. "Come on, show me around." James guided her through the lower-level rooms.

Maybeth opened the door to the third room and started to enter. It was a large, very tidy office. The wide redwood desk was adorned with small statues and a vase of fresh cut flowers. "Not much in here," Dr. said, trying to steer Maybeth back out. "Oh, no," she gently brushed his hand aside.

"This is where all that good advice germinates. I want to experience the 'aura'." James creased his brow and watched tentatively as Maybeth paced slowly into the room. She ran her fingers lithely along the edge of his desk - hefted one of the bronze busts - bent and smelled the array of flowers, her smile genuine and respectful. Near the desk was a custom-made chess table with 9" pieces moved about the board. "Do you play chess with yourself, James?" she teased, winking at him. "And sometimes I let myself win," he winked back. Maybeth giggled. "Smart and funny,"

A groggy Ashley padded around the corner and through the open doorway. "Hi Mommy," she said. "Hi James. I'm all rested. Can we play some games now?" Both Maybeth and James smiled at her. "I don't get to have 2 beautiful ladies in my house very often. I think we should celebrate." Ashley nodded, then said, "We could come here every day if that would help you, James. "

Chapter Forty-One

Reacting from anger

T HE FULL-LENGTH MIRROR HUNG on the closet door in Carla's tiny studio apartment. She was holding up various outfits, trying to decide what to wear to the dinner at Dr. Fuquan's house, when her cell phone chimed. Still modeling a pantsuit Carla was feeling great! Grinning, she chirped, "This is Carla." It seemed that since her days in the hospital - since the tremendous support and outpouring of love she had received, she couldn't stop grinning. Nearly every call was from someone in the class ... checking on her, making sure she was okay. "Hey, it's Wayne." the familiar voice replied.

Wayne had called more than all the others, but this time she detected something different in his voice ... a loneliness ... a depression... a fear or dread? "What is it?" her smile vanished.

The phone now mashed to her ear. "Where are you? What's the matter?" "Ha-ha," Wayne forced a laugh. "Nothin's the matter. I'm just checkin' on you." "No," Carla shot right back. "Something is bothering you. What is it? You tell me, right now!" "Hey," Wayne tried to lighten the mood. "I'm just making sure you'll be ready when I come by to get you." Caught off guard - again - Carla felt her face flush. "You know I said I could get there on my ..." "And I said I'm picking you up!"

"But ..." Carla protested, her eyes roaming her humble residence, her mind seeing the exterior of the rundown building. "NO buts, Carla," Wayne was insistent. "I'll be there at 5:30. You better be ready." "I'll ... I'll meet you ..." Carla tried one last evasion. "I'll be knocking on your door," Wayne assured her. "That's where we'll meet. Get up early so you can be all dolled up before I arrive. As quickly as the conversation began, it ended. Carla was torn. She could sense something was bothering Wayne, but her anxiety over him seeing where she lived overpowered what she knew she should do. "What kind of a friend am I?" she muttered to herself. "My friend needs me and all I can think of is being embarrassed." She picked up the phone - looked at it several moments - then flung it down on the bed.

Wayne clicked off from Carla, dropping his phone on the seat next to him. He kept his eyes on the road; his car speeding west on I-20, headed for Ft. Worth. The night before he had paced his house like a caged lion, trying to abate the fury that consumed him. He squeezed his eyes shut, but all he could see was the image of Father Murphy ... his round jowls sagging above him, demanding he continue... threatening him ... warning him of eternal purgatory if he ever told a soul.

"I can't live with this!" He had finally choked back the tears long enough to come to a decision. "Unless I resolve this, I can never move forward." Wayne had never been to the Cathedral in Fort Worth, but he drove there almost absent mindedly. He wasn't even aware he had parked and was walking into the large, spired building. His feet knew exactly where to go - to the same place the priest had taken him each time in Dallas - for their 'rendezvous'.

Opening the door, Wayne stepped into the living quarters. "This is my private resi..." Father Murphy gasped when he saw Wayne. The young man kneeling in front of the priest looked just as frightened as Wayne had been when he was forced into that position. "Hello Father," Wayne snarled the words. "Remember me?" "No!" the Priest shouted. "You get out of here - get out of here right...."

The first blow was so violent the cleric crumpled instantly to the floor. When the ambulance arrived - fifteen minutes later Wayne fled the scene - Father Murphy was unconscious. Three ribs were cracked, his left arm was broken, there were gashes and cuts across his face, and his nose was shattered. He would live, but he would never forget his final encounter with Wayne Wade. Each glance in the mirror would be a horrifying reminder. "We have a description of the assailant," the investigator interviewing the young man who witnessed the attack, told his Captain on the walkie-talkie. "Write it up," the captain instructed him "and put out an APB."

Wayne was spiraling. He was experiencing so many emotions at once fear, regret, terror, relief, and confusion. He thought that getting revenge would feel better. But it didn't. It felt horrible. It didn't take away the pain he had inside. It didn't remove the memories. It only added new ones. Wayne had to get control of himself. He took out his phone and called the one person he believed could help him. "Hello? This is Dr. Fuquan." said the man on the other end of the line. Wayne tells him that he is in trouble and needs to meet. "Of course, where are you?" responded Dr. Fuquan. He would always be available for those who needed him. This was something James promised himself he would always do.

Nervous and jittery, Wayne tries to explain his location to Dr Fuquan, but couldn't get it out. Dr Fuquan was concerned. He had never seen Wayne act this way. He asked again "Wayne where are you?" "I don't know ... I'm next to a William's chicken off i30 and Buckner." "Stay there! I'm on my way!" James pulls up to the location, Wayne gets out of his car and walks over to see the doctor. James opens his car door and knows immediately that something bad happened. Wayne was very disheveled, and his knuckles were busted and bleeding.

"What happened!?" Wayne recounts the details of what he just did. Upon hearing this James becomes very disappointed. He feels like he failed Wayne. "I thought I instructed you better. I thought you knew better. I just can't believe this..." James was more angry with himself, but Wayne didn't take it that way. After hearing James's disappointment, Wayne instantly becomes defensive. "I should have known you wouldn't understand!!" Wayne turns away and starts yelling.

"You don't get it!

"What the hell was I thinking?"

"You don't have a clue what I'm dealing with!"

"You just live your fancy, pampered life!"

"Man, Fuck this!"

"I'm out! Thanks for nothing!"

James reaches for Wayne's shoulder trying to calm him down. Wayne grabs his hand and forcefully throws it off.

"NO fuck you!" You don't know what it's like! I should have known you couldn't understand! Have you ever been sexually abused? Have you ever had any trauma? Man, you just collecting a paycheck!" Wade waves his hand dismissing James and turns to walk away. James is trigged by Wayne's aggression and loses his cool. He starts yelling, the veins in his neck bulging. As spit flies out of his mouth he lets loose.

"You don't know shit!! No!! I have never been sexually abused but trust me ... I know pain!" As he starts pounding on his chest, he continues. "My whole fucken life is trauma and pain!" A flashback of Otis on top of Martha's beaten and bloodied body flashes through James' mind. "You didn't spend 15 years in prison for a crime you didn't commit – a crime you had to watch!" Another image of James carrying Martha's lifeless body flashes. "You don't know what it feels like to watch your girlfriend be raped and murdered and you are helpless to do anything!"

James is unable to control his rage at this point. As James is yelling, he starts pointing aggressively at Wayne. "Who the fuck do you think you are to question me and my pain?!" The rage is boiling up inside him. Anger now exploding from the pain and hurt he has been harboring all these years. "Boy ..." as he gritted his teeth. "I was the one that failed to protect the people that I love! ... ME!" James continues to beat on his chest. A grisly image of Darwin's beaten body lying in a puddle of blood, flashes. "I may not have experienced exactly what you have but I know pain!"

Wayne is shocked! This is the first time he's seen Dr. Fuquan, enraged and out of control, he is speechless. For a split-second Wayne felt a shiver of fear. Never in his mind did he think he would be hearing what he just did. How? How did this rich and well put together doctor overcome all that? Wayne's shoulders fall and he leans against the car. James moves beside him ... silent. A few minutes passes and Wayne breaks the moment "I'm sorry, I had no idea." James understands, "That is intentional, I keep my past very private, people judge. They stay there for a while discussing James's past and how well he does, in fact, understand. Before leaving, Dr. Fuquan reiterates "What was said tonight stays between us right?" Wayne nods his head; they shake hands then embrace.

Chapter Forty-Two

An unexpected moment

"OH, MY GOODNESS," MAYBETH exclaimed, "look at the time. It's nearly three a.m. How did it get so late so fast?" Maybeth and James were seated on the couch in the living room. "I need to get home, or I'll never get up in time to get back here before the others arrive." "I have plenty of room," James suggested. "Three extra bedrooms ... You and Ashley should just stay the night. She's sleeping and it would be a shame to wake her, besides, you said her overnight bag was in the car." "It is," she confirmed, "but I don't have a thing." "There's a shower in each room," James reasoned. "I can throw your shirt and jeans in the washer while you're showering. No reason to go to such trouble when you're planning to be back in just a few hours anyway."

Maybeth smiled, "If you're sure you don't mind." "I insist," he answered, rising from the couch and taking her hand to pull her to her feet in front of him. Neither said a word. They stood - staring at each other. "I..." Maybeth finally whispered, "I don't have a nightshirt." Without taking his eyes off hers, James said, "I have a closet full of T-shirts. You can choose the one you want." Still gazing into his eyes, Maybeth slid her arm up his side, then tugged at the T-shirt James was wearing. "I choose ... this one." she whispered, leaning slightly forward, her breasts lightly grazing his firm chest. James swallowed hard. "This one?" "Uh-huh." she nodded, still staring into his eyes. Slowly James pulled the shirt over his head and held it out for her, wearing nothing but a white undershirt and pants, losing eye contact to look at his body.

"Wow!" she said. "Um James swallowed again, "I'll look in on Ashley while you're in the shower." Maybeth nodded, and slowly backed away, still looking James up and down. When she bumped into the wall behind her, she was so embarrassed, she left the room. Ashley was fine - sleeping soundly hugging a stuffed toy. James smiled at the innocence - the purity and wondered what it would have been like to be a father - to have a child depend on him and trust him and love him. James took a quick shower and put on his silk PJ's, walked to the kitchen to get a glass of wine and decided to sit down and play the piano Maybeth heard the music as she was drying off. She slipped on the extra-large T-shirt, letting it drop, nearly to her knees The neck gaped open, she followed the sound, walking into the living room where James sat on the piano, his back turned to her. The music seemed to flow effortlessly from his fingers a concerto, she thought. Maybe Beethoven or Bach. The grand piano seemed to be singing.

Silently she padded up behind him and laid her hand on his shoulder. "You never cease to amaze me doctor." she whispered. James finished the measure, then turning on the bench to face her. James could not imagine Maybeth being so sexy. A short petite blonde with wet hair, no panties and wearing his oversized V-neck shirt. The top is loose and low, when she leaned forward toward him, he could see everything She had the most perfect breasts with the prettiest pink nipples he had ever seen, but yet super soft. Instinctively his hands rose cupping her hips as she leaned closer to him, her head tilted, and her lips gently kissed his. James began to slowly rub his hands up her legs cupping her butt and then her breasts and without a word in one motion he put his hands around her waist while remaining seated and picked her up.

Maybeth's hands looped around his neck and pulled him closer, tighter. She wanted to feel his body. She needed to feel his masculinity! She was always curious and tonight her curiosity would be answered. Is it really like they say it is?? Would he really be more loving, caring and understanding? Their kiss deepened into a sweltering passion ... a ravenous lust. As he tasted and explored her body, he knew this was no one night stand. This was no lustful craving with a superficial woman, impressed only with his position or his possessions. From the first class, the first time he saw her and heard her voice, he wanted her- not as a trophy ... not as a physical conquest. He wanted all of her- her mind, her thoughts, her companionship. The touch of her fingers- the sensation of her hair and her body... oh yes, without a doubt he wanted her body.

He could feel her pressing back and forward as she glided her hand down his chest and slid it inside his PJs "Ooooh my James!" they both sighed together, still locked in a passionate kiss. Neither wanted a break. When their lips separated, they came right back together again- and again, savoring each other completely James brought his hands down to Maybeth's butt and lifted her in the air. Gently- as if she were an expensive rare chandelier. He sat her on top of the piano. Maybeth laid back and arched her back, opened her legs placing her feet on the piano keys as James slowly began kissing her feet and sucking her toes. James spread her legs apart over his head as wide as he could kissing his way up to her sweet spot. While still settled, he kissed and sucked, and licked her until a loud moan escaped her mouth.

She grabbed the back of his head with both hands as her body trembled. James stood up and released himself through the opening of his PJs, pulling Maybeth's body close to the edge of the piano with such gentleness, he slid himself slowly, into her, penetrating slow but going deeper and deeper with every stroke until he was completely in. Maybeth arched her back again moaning and moving her hips forward taking it all. James could not believe how wet Maybeth was, "Wow! You feel so incredible sweetie!" he continued looking down seeing her juices all over him! He continued sliding deeper while reaching to remove her shirt freeing her breasts as his lips met her nipples. He delicately circled them with his tongue before putting them entirely in his mouth. As he wrapped his arms around her legs pulling closer, Maybeth pulling him with her hands forcing him even deeper inside of her taking all of him with every stroke, satisfying the deep appetite she had. Setting herself free as she had never done before, so passionately, so completely.

James exploded and continued stroking for a while longer before slowly pulling himself out. "No, please don't take i t... please I'm still...!" Moaning as she touched herself while James was still inside of her. He could feel the pulse of her tender spot clenching around him. Hearing her moan and watching her play with herself was turning James on again, he began to get hard. The eruption they experienced together was enormously satisfying. But Maybeth wanted more! James kept stroking until he was completely hard again. Maybeth said, "Oooh babeee don't stop. I can't... I can't stop Cum...." She exploded all over James. While he was still erect, he slowly removed himself. She quickly sat on the piano stool before taking him in her mouth. "Muuh Mmmh, " with a mouthful before James stopped her and turned her around positioning her from behind, looking at her perfectly round butt.

Maybeth stood on her tip toes while James put his hands around her waist, moving closer until he found her sweet spot. Maybeth said, "Stop baby stop... I wanna do it!" She quickly thrusted her hips back, long stroking James while taking both hands and spreading herself apart so he could go deeper. James was in awe as he stood still watching his loins disappear with every thrust, removing his hands from her waist right before exploding deep inside her. They stayed together connected, clutching, kissing for several long minutes afterwards. When James could find his voice again, he said, "I ... I never experienced anything ...so magnificent ...so incredible! He slowly pulled out of Maybeth and sighed. "And never

ever did I imagine I would be with a white woman...not after what happened out there that night on the... "

Maybeth pressed her finger to his lips to hush him. "Evil isn't color coded," she said. "the color of a person's skin does not determine their virtue or their decency I hope you can look beyond my skin. just look at me see, the person I am, the person you have helped me become, the person who has loved you since she met you." She leaned forward to kiss him again. James watched her... naked body press against his again-felt her lips caress his mouth-felt a yearning, not only the deep carnal desire she stirred inside of her, but an inter twining of souls-complete unity of mind and body. Finally, for the first time -after all the years he had studied it and the thousands of sessions he had counseled on it...John Ferguson felt something he thought had passed him by. Though he had a quaint definition for it, he acted as the specialist to so many, but this was the first time he had experienced...love.

As John laid there, reminiscing about the amazing moment they just shared, he was afraid to fall asleep. Afraid of what he would do. He was afraid that he would have a PTSD episode and hurt Maybeth like he did Sarah. He would never forgive himself. It was a secret he never wanted to share with anyone. He never allowed anyone to get this close to him. He never allowed anyone to stay overnight. Not after what happened with Sarah. The one time he relaxed and let her fall asleep in his bed, the one time that he let his guard down, he broke his girlfriend's jaw in his sleep. It wasn't until she cried out in excruciating pain that he was suddenly awaken. John knew he had this problem. He was afraid to lose Maybeth.

He didn't want to say anything to Maybeth that would make her change her mind. He laid there growing anxious thinking about the moment he had to have this conversation. How could he explain why he was a danger to the woman he loved. PTSD post-traumatic stress disorder affected John as a result of all the trauma he had experienced. Martha's death, the many beatings he suffered in prison, the traumatic death of Darwin, losing his Mom and Dad, all this tormented John subconsciously and in his sleep, he lashed out. While he vowed to be a fighter on his feet. He never realized in his bed that he would become one as well. Countless times he had hit the walls and bars while sleeping in his cell. Regularly busting his knuckles, hands and feet was normal thing. Only for John to awaken and realize he was fighting himself.

The strange thing about John and his battle with PTSD is that John was always completely asleep and unaware of his actions. He thought about seeking help, but he was too afraid that if he did he would be put on medication. He was afraid of being judged and afraid that it would possibly affect his medical license or his practice. He prays and hopes that one day it would disappear as quickly as it came. He never had anyone to share his deepest secrets with. He could not bear to hurt Maybeth in any way. But he knew he could not stay awake for the rest of his life.

Chapter Forty-Three

A redefining moment

CARLA WAS PHYSICALLY SHUDDERING as she waited for Wayne to arrive, when the knock came, she was sure she would shrink away from embarrassment. Though she kept the interior neat -nearly immaculate-the building was old siding was falling off, drainpipes sagged, and the neighborhood! How could anyone risk coming here with the reputation these streets had? How can anyone like her when they saw where she lived?

"Hi." she meekly said, holding the door ajar only a few inches. I'm ready ... I'll just get my jacket." She started to close the door again, but Wayne pushed it open. That's when she saw him - his wrinkled clothes, disheveled hair, and drooping spirits. "Wayne!" She felt her concerns fly from her, "What is it? You look ... you look." He flung his arms around her, buried his head on her shoulder and wept. Carla didn't move, she let him sob then slowly raised her arms and pulled him to her. Something was wrong, she knew that, but what? And she also knew he would only tell her when he was ready.

Minutes passed by, Wayne letting his emotions flow from him while Carla held on to him like a lifeline. Gradually his embrace eased, and he created a separation. "You were right," he mumbled. "You... Dr. Fuquan ... all of you." "Wayne," Carla placed a hand on each side of his face and stared at him. "What are you talking about? What do you mean? What happened?" "Revenge," Wayne moaned and Carla gasped. "It's ... it's not fulfilling it's empty ... it's a lie... it's a big lie." "Oh, Wayne," Her heart was breaking. "Tell me ... tell me what you did.??"

In broken spurts, Wayne poured out his heart to the girl who only weeks ago swore she hated him. He told her about finding Father Murphy. He watched her eyes widen as he told her about the young boy the priest was abusing when he walked in. Carla clasped her hands to her mouth when Wayne described the assault. While she may have empathized with him and the past he carried, she remained silent, fully aware that any justification she gave him would only make her his enabler.

When he finished, Wayne raised his sad eyes and looked at her. "I got what I wanted... but when I left, on the ride home, I felt as dirty as he was. I had lowered myself to his level. I ... I almost couldn't live with myself, thinking I may be like him. Carla couldn't hold back this time. "You're not, Wayne," she cried. "You are not like him!" "What I did ... was just for me. That's all I thought about was satisfying my anger and hatred!" He shook his head. "Now what am I going to do? The police will be looking for me." Carla hugged him, pulling him tight to her. "We're going to Dr. Fuquan's." she said with authority, still clinging to him. "Then then you'll go to the police, and I'll go with you. If you want me to... and whatever happens, you'll be my friend and we'll get through this together. I won't abandon you."

Wayne's shoulders were jerking as he tried to control his sob. "I don't deserve a friend like you." She softly kissed the top of his head. "Everyone deserves a friend." She waited a minute, then said, "And everyone deserves a turkey dinner on Thanksgiving- especially when it's shared with friends. Are you ready to take me?" "You really mean it?" Wayne asked, wiping his face on his sleeve "You'll really come with me to the police station?" "I feel honored to go with you." Carla told him. "That's what friends do ... and you're the best friend I've ever had." Wayne choked back more tears, regained his composure, bent his elbow so she could loop her hand through it. "Your chariot awaits you, beautiful lady." He said, and they left arm in arm.

Chapter Forty-Four

A pleasant surprise

"SOMETHING IS DEFINITELY VERY different," James thought to himself, blinking open his eyes. "And it's very, very nice." He grinned and looked down at Maybeth curled tightly under his arm, her head resting on his chest. The grin grew into a full-forced smile? One he couldn't remove if he wanted to. He gently ran his finger over the smooth cheek bone-along her jawline down to her shoulder, then cupped her breast. Maybeth stirred slightly, a moan of pleasure as she snuggled closer "Why have I avoided this all these years?" James asked, but he knew the answer. "I had to meet Maybeth. This could not have happened with anyone else." Maybeth rotated her head to look up at him. "I'm falling in love with you James." she sighed.

"I beat you to it," he continued caressing her. "I know I'm in love with you. I think I may have known for weeks, but last night confirmed it." Maybeth felt the panic return. "I...

James when you ... " James could see the apprehension in her face. "What, when, what?" Her eyes closed and she prayed she could tell him and that he would somehow understand. "It was it was 3 years ago. I Leon wanted I ... I had an abortion. I let them kill my child," she couldn't open her eyes. She couldn't face him. James pulled her closer. "We all have a past my love," he said. "I could never hold that against you." "But" Maybeth's chin dug into his chest, "the surgery some- thing went wrong and I ... I cannot have more children."

James let her weep a moment, then he slipped his thumb under her chin and lifted it so she was looking at him. "We have Ashley," he said. "She is more than I ever dreamed of. She will be the object of our affection, and we can help others, too. Please, Maybeth, now that I've found you - that we've found each other - let's celebrate our love. It is so rare in the world today. And we have been given this priceless gift. Let's start anew ... you and me. Let's begin our lives today - together."

A crooked smile cracked across her face, dripping tears from her eyes. "I don't deserve you," she said. "Someone so wonder- ful and so full of love. But ... I do NOT intend to let you go, either." "And I promise I will never leave." Maybeth leaned up to kiss him - deeply. Then she rolled on top of him, straddling him. Her beautiful body only added to the affection he was feeling. Once on top, she moved over him, taking him deep inside her as he embraced her. She looked down at his perfect face, feeling him moving inside her, and she was sure no one in all the world had ever felt such passion before.

James blinked - a long blink - and when he opened his eyes, she was still there. It was no dream no mirage. He, too, was positive he was the first man to ever experience a love so deep. He knew without reservation that he, too, had been changed by the class, that he would never go back to being the private recluse he had been, and that he would fight with every ounce of energy in his soul to keep Maybeth and Ashley. Just as the explosion was rising in him uncontrollably again, Maybeth gasped deeply and loudly several times, then lunged forward, kissing him deeply - holding her lips to his while the ecstasy filled both of them. When the trembling subsided, she opened her eyes, smiled, and whispered, "I love you, James Fuquan."

They laid there for a moment. Maybeth grew quiet and James notices "What's wrong?" Maybeth, apprehensive to divulge what was on her mind, decided it would be best to be open and honest. "Who is John Ferguson?" "James' throat grew thick and tight, after clearing his throat, he managed to speak, "I have a past," he finally said, revealing a secret very few people knew. As she sat - in rapt attention - John Ferguson now James Fuquan told her the story of a young man unjustly convicted who spent 15 years in prison. He told her of the deception that gave him his freedom, the diligent hours of studying and the stigma that followed him, and the doors that would never open to him because of his past. Finally, he told her about Clay Stephenson and his assistance in changing his name. "I'm embarrassed I had to do that," he admitted. "But I will never be ashamed of the work I do or the lives I have encountered along the way. I never would have met you or the others if I was still John Ferguson."

A tear bubbled from Maybeth's eye and raced down her cheek. "Then," she announced, "you did the right thing. Because you saved my life and the others in our class, too. You should tell them, James, I needed you, I know they need you too." James was feeling a fear he thought he had buried. Could he risk exposing himself who he really was .. to all of them? "It's up to you, James," Maybeth looked deeply into his eyes. "But if it will help ... I will be right beside you ... if you want me to. If you want to tell them." She reached for his hand, and he clutched hers.

Chapter Forty-Five

Being thankful

"WILL THERE BE MORE of you?" the security guard at Manhattan Estates asked when Brian and Jennifer coasted to a stop next to him and introduced themselves. Brian slipped his arm around Jennifer, looked up at the guard and said, "There will never be another one of her. God broke the mold when he created perfection." Jennifer grinned and snuggled her head deeply into his shoulder while the security guard rolled his eyes. "I was told to expect 8 guests for Dr. Fuquan. Six have shown up this morning, however two arrived yesterday and never logged out. I was wondering if the 8 included those two."

"Two stayed the night?" Brian asked with a suspicious lilt. Jennifer sat up as well, both of them sporting trite smiles when the guard nodded. "Who were they ... the two that spent the night?" The guard consulted his log. "A Maybeth Simmons and a child named Ashley." "Umm hmm, " Brian hummed. He twerked an eyebrow at Jennifer, then back at the sentry. "No. I don't think you need to expect anyone else. I believe we're all here now." "Thank you," the guard almost saluted. He opened the huge gate and Brian, and Jennifer followed their map to the house. Dr. Fuquan received a call from the front gate and met them at the door with the rest of the group close behind him.

When they entered - holding hands - Kevin gave his friend a gentle punch on the shoulder. "I had a feeling about you two," he said. "Looks like I was right." "Classroom romances," Dr. Fuquan chided them. "Actually, statistics say they are much more likely to succeed than workplace attractions. In the long run." Brian smiled like the Cheshire cat. "You'd be the one to know about that."

"Yes," the doctor replied, questioning the way Brian kept nodding his head slowly and mumbling, "Umm hmmm." When he continued, the rest of the students began to crease their foreheads and look from one to the other. "What is it, Brian?" Wayne finally asked. "You look like you swallowed a secret." "Well," Brian drug out the word, "maybe our distinguished teacher - and overnight host - might want to tell you," He shot a darting look from James to Maybeth and back. James was befuddled. Very unprofessionally his mouth opened like a loose hinge and remained that way. Maybeth stepped forward, grinning from ear to ear. She looped her arm around his waist and told the group, "If he's too shy to kiss and tell, I'm not." She hugged James.

"We cooked more than turkey yesterday," she cooed. "We did a little cake baking too, and the icing ... well ... a lady never talks." Congratulations and hugs fell around them like confetti. Everyone was clutching Brian and Jennifer and James and Maybeth. When Maybeth finally led them to the formal dining room, everyone caught their breath and gawked in amazement at the array of food dishes and the gigantic turkey waiting to be carved. Maybeth was the excited, gracious hostess, showing each person to their assigned seats, then sitting down next to James, her hand slipping under the tablecloth and resting on his thigh, in a comfortable, natural manner.

"Thank you for coming," James addressed the shining faces looking back at him. He couldn't help but marvel at their radiance - at the sparkle in every eye and the impression of peace they seemed to convey such a stark contrast to the angry, sulking, insecure individuals he had met just 3 months earlier. "My home has never looked or felt better than it does today." With a wide grin he added, "It is decorated with something more precious than fine furnishings, rarer than a Rembrandt painting, and more valuable than gold and silver. Today it is adorned with friends." Small hugs were shared with the ones they sat next to before James spoke again. "Since this is Thanksgiving Day," he said, "I thought it would be appropriate if each of us took a minute to express our gratitude for whatever we are thankful for this year, if you want to. Would anyone like to go first?"

Jennifer didn't hesitate. "I'm thankful," she said, rising to her feet, "for so, so much. I have been reinstated at school and I can return next semester." When the raucous cheer died down, Jennifer continued, "I have made changes and learned things that will make me a better person forever. The man I adore and cherish and who makes me better in every way, also loves me. I couldn't be any happier than I am right now." Before James could ask for the next volunteer, Brian stood up. "The good news just keeps coming," he beamed. "My agent called, and I have a spot on the Cowboys' practice squad, which could ... I say could lead to a roster position in the future." "I want tickets," Kevin deadpanned and the congratulations were mixed with laughter.

"And," Brian went on, "I too, have found power to rid my life of the toxins that afflicted me for so long ... anger and hatred and revenge. I promise, as long as I live, I will never go back to the man I was. There is really no chance, no fate and no destiny that can get me to abandon my future." After a brief silence, Kevin asked, as if on cue, "Aren't you going to say anything about Jennifer after all that good stuff she made up about you?"

Jennifer waved her hand amid more laughter. "No." she said, "He doesn't need to." "Oh, yeah," "Brian cleared his throat, interrupting her. Then, slowly, he slid off his feet and onto one knee. Seemingly out of nowhere he produced a small box. Opening it, the diamond sparkled like he was holding fire. With tears pouring down Jennifer's face, Brian took her hand. "I love you, Jennifer Potter. Will you make me the happiest man who ever lived and marry me for the rest of our lives?" "Yes!! Oh, my Yes!!!" Jennifer slobbered and blubbered. After slipping the ring on her finger, she threw her arms around his neck and kissed him.

James leaned over to Maybeth and whispered, "He can only be the second happiest man alive. I got number one all wrapped up." "Don't know how anyone could top that," Carla sighed as she rose to her feet. "But I am thankful for so much and I must share it with you. I've thought so much about the feelings I've had - the changes I've felt - the love you have given me. I could never repay you because I realized something while I was lying in the hospital bed. You -each of you - are angels sent to me from God above. There is no other conclusion I could draw. And I plan to dedicate my life to Him in an effort to, to thank Him for sending me the angels that are seated around this table today. Truly, I was lost and not I'm found, and you. were my guideposts. I hope someday, to be as good to others as you have been to me."

When Carla sat down, Kevin popped up. "I been called a lot of things in my life," he said, "and I've done a lot of gambling, and I would have bet everything I have that I would never, in my life, be called an angel." He glanced a smile at Carla while the group chuckled. "Now, having said that, I want to thank each of you. You are the family I never had. I can see light and hope in your eyes, and that's what I want people to see in mine. Thank you."

"I guess it's no secret," Maybeth almost giggled as she stood, dragging James's hand up with her. She kissed it lightly, basking in the warmth of those around her and in the love of a man who truly loved her. "I could not have imagined this scene a few months ago. I was broken ...no," she corrected herself, "I was shattered. My life was spinning out of control. And now..." Her voice cracked and she heaved a deep breath, "now I'm the luckiest woman in the world. I lost my dear daughter Amber, and I was so empty. Our family was leaking love and affection as fast as a broken dam leaks water." She smiled down at James. "Then this man - this incredible, wise, loving forgiving man, came into my life - into our lives - and now each of us has a family. We have each other, we have a future - a bright and glorious future ... and I have something so much more delicious than Dutch apple pie. I have love. However much more time God gives me on Earth, I need to spend it loving everyone ... and especially James and Ashley."

Tears were being dabbed from every eye. Breaking the silence, Wayne stood up slowly. "I guess it's my turn," he mumbled, his head down. "You have all inspired me and I adore each of you, but I've let you down." Heads were shaking but Wayne held up his hand. "I have," he insisted, and proceeded to explain what he had done to Father Murphy the night before. "But" he held up a finger, "Tomorrow, accompanied by the best friend I have ever had, Carla Warfield," he paused as each head turned to look at Carla, "I'm going to the police station and turn myself in. I'll accept the punishment because I've learned firsthand, that life is way too sweet to carry around the heavy baggage of revenge and hatred. Carla has promised to visit me if I go to jail."

Carla nodded and the others voiced their commitments as well. "Knowing I have that support," Wayne swallowed to hold back his emotions, "and that love from you - my family - makes me the most grateful person in the room." He quickly sat down and buried his head in Carla's shoulder. She patted him tenderly, the room suspended in reverent silence.

James took one last deep breath, touched Maybeth's hand, then rose to his feet. "I've seldom seen such courage," he said, looking at Wayne, "It has given me the strength to come out from behind a rock where I've been hiding for two decades." With, everyone looking at him, James recounted his story. 'My real name is John Ferguson." he began. "I spent 15 years in maximum security at Texas Department of Corrections, for a crime I did not commit. Even though I was innocent, I was embarrassed and so I changed my name to avoid exposure of who I really am. Now, for the first time, I am revealing that long held secret. The love I have felt within this group, and the love I have found in the arms of the most beautiful woman in the world, has made me ashamed of the hypocrisy I lived under, and it has made me excited - thrilled - alive for the first time in my life."

He chuckled, then squeezed Maybeth's hand, and glanced at Ashley. "I'm going to be a Daddy - to that precious little girl. And I'm coming home every evening to a love that makes me pinch myself to believe it is real. This is truly a Thanksgiving Day. All this time, I thought I was the teacher, and it turns out that you have been teaching me."

He stood a moment in silence, then said, "This food won't last forever. I think it's time we did some eating. " "Wait!" Ashley cried out, "I didn't get a turn." Grinning, James ceded the floor to the precocious 5-year-old. "My apologies, Princess. Please tell us what you're thankful for today." "Well," Ashley pooched her lips, "I'm thankful that I got to make the Jell-o." The giggles lightened the mood in the room. "And," Ashley said in a confident voice, spreading her arms wide. "I'm thankful that we all love each other because love is what makes a family and my family got broken so now, I have a great big new family and I think we should have lots more meals together as a family." James smiled. "Out of the mouths of babes," he said. The serenity was palpable ... and contagious. Everyone felt it. "Now," James said, "If you don't mind, I'd like to say grace, because I am anxious to find out what kind of cook this beautiful lady is. "

Chapter Forty-Six

In search of a new life

"SURE SEEMS QUIET WITH everyone gone, Maybeth said as they loaded the dishwasher together. James grabbed her from behind, swooping his hand to smother her breasts. He leaned close and spoke into her ear, "I know a way we can make it a lot noisier in here." Maybeth giggled, rotated around, reached her arms up and hugged his neck. "That's a joyful noise I expect this house to hear a lot from now on." Her sultry voice tickled his lips. "OK, then!" James wiggled his eyebrows. "But not now," she patted his rear. "Right now, we need to get this kitchen cleaned up and I have to take Ashley to a birthday party and get some things from the house."

"How about we make some of that joyful noise," he winked and arched an eyebrow, "And I'll clean up the kitchen my-self while you're gone." "Umm," she rubbed herself against him. "Sure, sounds tempting, but how about I help with the dishes, then take Ashley to the party. It's a slumber party," Maybeth winked, "she's staying the night." James broke into a wide grin. "So, it would be just the two of us all night alone in the house." Maybeth nodded seductively. "And there are a lot of rooms that need to hear the sounds of love, don't you think?" "My lady," he grabbed a dishtowel, "Let's get these dishes done. I have some preparing to do, getting four rooms ready for romance will take a little time. But," he quickly caught himself, "Don't just stand there, hurry back here." She raised a leg and rubbed it on the inside of his thigh. "You can count on it," she said. An hour later, Maybeth and Ashley were preparing to leave. James stepped out into the porch and noticed the drizzling rain. "Change of plans he announced follow me."

"James," Maybeth protested "Hush," he picked her up in his arms. "You're taking my car. This cargo is too precious to me, and those roads could get nasty." Ashley padded along behind as Maybeth hugged James like a teenager on her first date, kissing his neck as he walked. He didn't set her down until Ashley had opened the door to the garage. "This is a Range Rover," he said, walking up to the nearest car. "The safest passenger vehicle on the highway." Maybeth was staring at the other car - the restored 1969 GTO. "James," she spoke softly, "is this?" "Yes," he answered in a whisper. "I'll never part with it .. and I'll never drive it again. It's brought me nothing but bad luck." Ashley tried to open the door to the Range Rover. "What about my car seat?" she asked.

James smiled. "I'll go get it with you while your Mommy backs the car out and meets us out front." He took her hand in his. He showed Maybeth a few of the features of the Range Rover, then scooped up the giggling Ashley. "Meet you out front," he called out, jogging back through the house. The car seat was quickly installed, and James leaned in for one more kiss. "I'm going to miss you." he said. Maybeth opened her eyes slowly. "I'm already missing you." James stood in the driveway until the car disappeared around the corner, then trudged back to the house.

He had spent years without her and thought his life was complete. Now, after less than 5 minutes, he knew it would be forever empty without Maybeth in it. Reaching for the door-knob, he heard his cell phone ring. Absentmindedly he pulled it out. "Dr. Ferguson," he said. "Ferguson? Oh..." Maybeth sighed, "I was looking for Dr. Fuquan." James perked up in-stantly. "That's me!" He shouted like a kid getting his favorite toy for Christmas. "I miss you." Maybeth's perky voice sang in his ear. "And I love you."

Oh, how he loved that woman. "I should demand you come straight back here." he tried to sound stern, "and give me another kiss." "Mmmmm," Maybeth purred, "wait 'til you see the kisses I have planned for you when get back." James felt as light as a whirlwind. "I think I can match you, kiss for kiss." he nearly slurred his words. "I'm counting on it," Maybeth whispered so seductively he thought he could feel her warm breath through the telephone "I love you." Maybeth finished her sentence. "Say it again," James begged. "I so love hearing it." "I love you ... I love you... I love you!" Maybeth told him. "And I'll be back soon. You better be ready..."

Suddenly Maybeth screamed! Then James heard tires screeching and crunching metal then the line went dead. "Maybeth?" James held the phone out in front of him. "Maybeth!" he screamed. "Maybeth!" Then, like a sprinter bursting from the starting blocks, James exploded off the steps, sprinting with all his might, terror rushing through him. He rounded the corner, screaming at the gate guard who was standing next to a car - the wide gate just opening. James shot through the gap at a dead sprint.

When he cut around the corner, a block from the gate, his entire body shook, his legs went weak, his stomach nearly retched. In the middle of the intersection his Range Rover was crumpled - a large pickup truck had smashed head on into the driver's door. Before he reached the car, he could see blood splatters on the windshield. Throwing caution aside, James leaped across the mangled hood and plunged down as close as he could get to the smashed door. Ashley was in her car seat, unhurt, but crying. Maybeth was scrunched between the ruptured door panel and the console. Her eyes were bobbing lifelessly.

"Maybeth... Maybeth," he squeezed his arm through the broken glass, chards ripping to his skin. "James ..." the weak voice responded. "James," her eyes closed "No!" James shouted. He called 911 on his phone. "Hurry," he hollered. "Please hurry," he said again after giving the dispatcher the location of the collision. He tossed his phone aside and ran his arm through the broken glass a second time, finding Maybeth's arm. "No, Maybeth," he pleaded. "Not after I just found you. No! no!" He found her limp limb and felt for a pulse. He couldn't find one.

Chapter Forty-Seven

When faith stands up

POLICEMEN HAD TO NEARLY arrest James to get him to back away from the car. The Jaws of Life dug quickly, tearing away the metal in pieces as they scrambled to extract Maybeth from the vehicle. Paramedics and an ambulance were already waiting - hoping for a chance to save her life ... praying she was still alive when they got her out. James was holding Ashley so tight he thought he might crush her in his arms. He tried to force the thoughts from his mind .. what if Maybeth didn't make it. Could he take Ashley? Would the court let him?

No - no - he pushed those thoughts away. Maybeth had to make it she had to. After so many years alone, then finding her ... she couldn't leave him, not now, not this way. James tried to watch closely as Maybeth's unconscious body was finally strapped to the stretcher and placed into the ambulance. Three EMT's scrambled in behind her, the doors shut, and the whirring scream of the siren tore through the evening air. James removed Ashley's car- seat and an officer gave him a ride home. The keys to Maybeth's car were in her purse - somewhere. He didn't feel comfortable digging in her purse, so her car was not an option at the moment. He hesitated only a second, then strapped the car seat into the GTO, fired it up, and sped off for the hospital.

The GTO purred like a kitten, screeching to a halt in the parking lot. "If I lose Maybeth, too, while I'm driving this car, I'll push it over a cliff," he swore. "Maybe with me in it." He would have called someone - he had a 'family' now - but his phone was somewhere - he couldn't remember where he had thrown it. All he could think about was Maybeth.

When James felt he had no place left to turn, he fell on his knees. "Please, God," he muttered, "I can't live without her. Please don't take her from me." The doctor met him in the waiting room, where James had been pacing so fiercely the admitting nurse worried about his condition. "She's in surgery," the doctor informed him. "Then she's alive," James nearly broke down, a relief sweeping over him like he had never felt before. In a nasally voice, the Dr. said, "Clinically, she was dead when she arrived. We managed to get her heart restarted and she was rushed to the OR. All we can do now is wait." And wait he did. BY 8:00 p.m., he realized he couldn't keep Ashley up all night.

He needed to call for help. But who? He didn't know any of Maybeth's friends or Ashley's. He didn't even know who the foster family was that had been caring for Ashley. In his mind he heard Ashley's voice, "We're a family now." By 9:00 p.m. all 5 of them were in the waiting room. Jennifer and Carla were tending to Ashley. Brian, Kevin and Wayne were sitting with James. The teacher /student barrier no longer existed. They were no longer just friends, now they were family. Doing what family does, supporting each other in a time of tragedy and need.

It was 3:37 a.m. when an exhausted doctor came through the swinging doors. Ashley was asleep on a small roll-away cot the nurses had provided. The other 6 leaped to their feet and rushed him. The doctor's sad, tired eyes were drooping - his shirt soaked in blood and perspiration. "She's alive," he said. "More than that, it's up to her. How badly she wants to pull through this. We'll know more in the morning."

"It is morning, Doc, " Kevin reminded him. The doctor forced a grin "You should go get some sleep. Come back around noon." "I want to see her," James demanded. "She's my. .... my fiancé. I want to see her." The doctor looked at him a moment, then nodded. "Just for a minute, though there's not much to see but bandages, tubes and needles." James followed the doctor, covered himself with sterile clothing, and booties, and walked into the ICU. Girding up his strength, he walked to the bedside. Maybeth, her tiny body broken and bruised, lay as still as a rock. James touched her hand then bent over the railing and kissed her. "I love you, Maybeth," he said. "I'll be waiting for you to wake up my darling. I'll never stop waiting." When he told the others of her condition, they too vowed to stay until she awoke ... if she awoke.

Chapter Forty-Eight

One step at a time

I T WAS LATE SATURDAY afternoon when the doctor came to the waiting room where 6 adults and a child had taken up residence. Every update for 2 days had been the same "no change." They looked up at the doctor, anticipation and worry etched in their faces. The doctor smiled. They hadn't seen that before. "She's awake," he said, igniting a chorus of cheers and jubilant dancing. "She's asking for somebody named James." He grinned at James. "She'd like to see him. That he promised to be here when she woke up."

James sprung forward, almost passing the doctor who still guarded the door." Can we come, too," Brian asked. "We're all family." The doctor eyed the eclectic group, then remembering how none of them would leave the hospital until Maybeth woke up, he clenched his lips tight and nodded. "But just for a minute. Too much too soon wouldn't be." His words were drowned out by the stampede. Six people and a child rushed for the sterile clothing. Minutes later the group was allowed into the ICU. Cautiously they stepped to her bed. "We're here my love," James whispered.

Maybeth's eyes fluttered open, and she looked up - at 6 figures covered from head to toe in green - even their faces were obscured by the sanitary masks. "James?" she whispered weakly. When James identified himself, Maybeth softly said, "Sorry about your car." James smiled. "I have another," he said. "Turns out it's not bad luck after all. It brought me back to you. In fact, I think everything is just about perfect as soon as you get home." "Home?" Maybeth breathed out the word. "Our home," James said. "The home of Mr. and Mrs. James Fuquan, if you'll have me." A tear welled in Maybeth's eye. "Yes!" she managed to say. James squeezed her hand. "Now, you just need to get well. I've waited a long time to find you, and I thought I lost you. I won't ever lose you again. You hear me?" Maybeth's hand wiggled to the railing, and she clutched his fingers and said... "You're the Doctor."

A little while passed before the doctor returned to the room and notified everyone it was time to leave. Maybeth needed to rest. "Will she be released tonight?" James inquired. "Unfortunately, no, we need to run some more tests. But hopefully tomorrow she will be well enough to be discharged." The doctor informed James as he left the room. Everyone said their goodbye and gave her hugs and headed out. James straggled behind and sits on the bed and kisses her forehead. "I am ready to start my life with you. You need to get better and come home." Maybeth quietly replies "Home ... I love the sound of that – I'll be home tomorrow." James took Ashley's hand, and they walked out. "I love you mommy." As James and Ashley left he said goodbye and thank you to everyone who was there. James took Ashley home to put her to bed and decided he should call it a night as well.

As James was leaving the hospital, he didn't realize he had parked in the farthest parking lot. He kept Ashley close. It wasn't lit very well and some of the overhead lights here flickering While he and Ashley walked to the car - Ashley asked, "Can I make Jell-o?" "Sure, we can tomorrow. We can make some and bring it to your mom." James answered. "Yay! I wanna make red Jell-o with fruit in it!" While they were distracted talking about Jell-o, James failed to notice they were being approached by 4 guys. The shortest guy spoke first. "What up schoo'?" James calmly replies. "How are you doing?" The second guy yells out "Let me hold somethin'!" James replies, "Pardon me?" The men moved closer aggressively, closing the distance between them and James and Ashley. James recognizes their change in body language and pushes Ashley behind him to protect her. The second guy repeats

"Let me hold somethin'!" James aggressively says, "We're just trying to get to my car. But if you really wanna hold somethin', you can hold DEEZ NUTS!!"

Suddenly the tallest guy moved swiftly to the front, pulled out a knife and snapped it open. James seeing this turns defensive and immediately strikes the guy closest to him with a fast right and shattered his nose. James pushes Ashley farther behind him to keep her safe between him and the car. The guy with the knife charges at James yelling loudly! James kicked him in the balls and quickly punched him in the face. The assailant drops the knife and immediately falls to the ground grabbing himself. The other two men rushed at James. James defends himself and protects Ashley by throwing blow after blow, annihilating the other two men. James hit one of the guys so hard with a right hook that he shattered the guy's eye socket and knocked his eyeball out!

James continues to deliver multiple punches hitting the final guy with a right hook and coming back with a straight left. He throws another right, grazing the top of the car. James quickly thought "Man I'm getting rusty— I need to set up and practice some hay bales." The last guy scrambles up and tried to retreat. "I'll be dammed if anyone is going to harm my daughter!" James yelled. James is now the aggressor. James quickly tripped the fleeting man. Yelling at him "YOU

WANNA HOLD SOMETHIN'??! YOU WANNA HOLD SOMETHIN'??! As James pummels him with blow after blow breaking his ribs. The guy was begging him to stop. James realized he had left Ashley at the car. Leaving the guy unconscious, he got up to grab Ashley and they quickly drove off.

As Wayne and Carla were walking to his car. Wayne had a quick thought about out turning himself in tomorrow. Afraid of the unknown. He wasn't sure what to expect, however he knew that taking responsibility for his actions was the right thing to do. Wade wanted to be a better man. He knew he had to step out of his comfort zone. He was anxious to get it over and done with and get back to his new life with his new family. This was a new feeling for him and he never wanted it to end. But he knew the quicker he turned himself in the quicker he could return home to start his new life with Carla.

Chapter Forty-Nine

Love doesn't walk away

JAMES AWOKE AT 7AM a little later than usual, he got out of bed and went to wash his face and noticed his hands were bloody and swollen. James tried to remember what happened. As he washed the blood from his hands and fingers, he pondered what might have transpired. He relived the moments leaving the hospital and putting Ashley to sleep. He walked into his room and saw blood all over his wall and headboard. As James was walking back in the room, he realized his right foot was really sore. It dawned on him – he realized he had an episode - the 4 thugs were in his dreams-and James had been fighting in his sleep ... James didn't remember any of it! He cleaned the blood off the wall and the headboard and changed his sheets to hide the scene. As he limped around that morning, he continued to wonder what happened to his foot - not remembering that in his sleep he kicked one of his attackers but instead it was the footboard to his bed. James makes his coffee and goes to his great room for his morning meditation. He begins to think about all the trauma he has survived and overcome.

His mind flashbacks to Martha's body covered in blood, the red necks, his father dying, his mother's broken heart. Memories of seeing his best friend Darwin's dead body, flashes of the prison fights, the puddles and puddles of blood, blood on the walls, blood on the floors, blood on the ceiling and all the countless attempts on his life. He is quickly overcome with emotions - grateful to have survived it all. James begins to think about Maybeth and the accident she was in and how thankful he is to God that she survived. It was overwhelming, James dropped to his knees and began to pray. He began asking God to remove the sounds he always heard - from prison - the sounds of men taking their last breath. The gurgling blood sound of a father, a brother, a son ... never going home. Feeling paralyzed not being able to reach out and help them because he had to protect himself. He continues to pray and asks God to clear his mind of the sounds, the thoughts and the flashbacks. He asks God to remove those sounds and scenes that make him fight at night.

The sun coming up brought him out of his meditation. James got up and got ready to bring Maybeth home. "Jell-o! We have to make the Jell-o!" James bandaged his hands before going to wake up Ashley. They make Jell-o together just as she wanted. James was really enjoying his new role as a dad. While they were making the Jell-o, Ashley noticed his bandages "What happened to your hands?!" James not wanting to answer, changes the topic. "Look at the time! We have to go pick up your mom!" They finish the Jell-o and head to pick up Maybeth. Maybeth was escorted to the front entrance by her nurse when James arrives. Once home James did all he could to make Maybeth comfortable. They relaxed together as a family the rest of the day. James had prepared a casserole while Ashley made the Jell-o so dinner preparation that night didn't take long. Maybeth was exhausted and James knew it was best to get her settled in bed. Nighttime falls, James is once again terrified about potentially having an episode. He crawls gently in bed next to Maybeth, doing his best to stay awake and keep her safe.

Sleep came quickly for James no matter how hard he tried to stay awake. Maybeth is suddenly startled from her sleep by James screaming.

"Keep talking and I'll punch you in the mouth!"

"You must think imma punk or somethin'!"

"Come at me then!"

"James?!! Maybeth calls out.

"I ain't tryin' to do no talkin'!"

"Git your punk ass on then!"

"James!!" Maybeth exclaims!

James continues to yell holding a conversation by himself. He is having a PTSD episode. He yells out again!

"Hey mother fucker!!" and starts barking like a dog. "WOOF WOOF!!"

James begins violently kicking, then in an unexpected jolt, starts swinging in the air left and right - left - right! Maybeth is terrified! She doesn't know what's happening! Maybeth quickly moves her injured, bruised body, she stumbles out of bed and turns on the light - James continues to lash out! She notices his eyes are closed! She begins to yell at him again.

"James! James what's going on!? JAMES!!"

James comes to and in a calm soft tone asks, "What's wrong baby? Are you okay?" As if he doesn't know what just happened! Maybeth responds, "What were you doing? Are you okay? You were fighting! Who were you fighting?" "Can we talk about this tomorrow?" he asks. "James, please we need to talk about this now I am worried about you!" Maybeth urges, James quickly realizes he was fighting in his sleep and is now forced to become more vulnerable than he ever has before. This love he has for Maybeth is worth it. He begins to tell her about his PTSD and all about the trauma he has experienced. "You were barking ... barking like a dog! What was that?! Maybeth curiously asked. James had to explain to her, that in prison, which was the troop call after riots for the aligned groups to see how many of their 'soldiers' were still standing. It was a way for them to judge the severity of the casualties to their group. Often there were walls separating the room and they would have a special call for each group to identify one another. The 'barking' was a dominance call for the blacks to know how many were left standing and to establish a victory.

Maybeth encourages James to seek help. He explains to her the reasons why he has been so private and hesitant in the past. He is concerned about his medical license and doesn't want to take medication or have this affect his work or practice. He refuses to have something like in his medical records. Together they decide the best thing for them to do now, is to monitor his sleep patterns and determine the best plan of action ... one step at a time.

It has been 6 weeks since the anger management class ended. Carla, Jennifer, Brian, Wayne and Maybeth all passed with flying colors. Judge O'Brien was very pleased with their progress. Despite the incident with Sam and Thruman, the judge felt the program was a success. Maybeth continued to monitor James's night time behavior. She has contacted multiple companies in regards to his PTSD. She spent many hours during her recovery doing research. She wanted to learn as much as she could in order to be helpful to James and his healing process. However, James's symptoms did not seem to be improving. Maybeth had become too scared to sleep in the same bed. James is afraid of hurting Maybeth. They agree to sleep on the opposite ends of the bed, placing pillows between them, to create a buffer zone. That seemed to help for a while. Unfortunately, James continued without warning to yell and fight in his sleep. This would always startle Maybeth awake and the lack of sleep was starting to take its toll.

U RGENT MESSAGE FOR ALL VICTIMS OF SEXUAL ASSAULT

You may feel ashamed and isolated or that you put yourself in a position to be sexually assaulted. Even if all this is true, that doesn't' give any one the right to abuse you ... no means no! Stop means just that, STOP!! How do you forgive and release your assailant when he or she has never been punished or held accountable for their dirty deeds?? By choosing to be happy. It's not easy letting go of the pain. You have the right to be angry, but don't be ashamed to ask for help, you're not alone. Are you afraid to trust but desperate for help? Sometimes we have to give up our right to be right, just to get past the pain. Don't ever consider taking matters into your own hands. Untamed anger can and will cause you a lot of trouble. Instead, pray about it. Ask God to help you forgive the jerk that caused you so much pain. It's not about how many times you have fallen, it's not about how you fell, it's about how you got up ... let me help you. Let me be your voice ... get behind me ... let me fight for you. I will stand with you and together we will make a change!! I have never been abused personally, but the woman I love has. That day changed our lives forever! I took matters into my own hands seeking revenge in her honor. I knew it wasn't the right thing to do, but I wanted him to feel the same way he made her feel, hopeless, helpless and afraid. I played a small role in this book as Kevin. I'm the first to admit that I haven't always made the best decisions and sometimes my untamed anger got the best of me. I'm not proud of my past, but through the journey I have grown to become the man I am today, with God's grace and my truth, I want to bring hope, peace, joy, and restoration to your life. Stolen moments are real, and they happen every day ... this is not just a book, it's a movement!

I am strong because being strong is my only option!!